Step Up
and
F.O.C.U.S
(Follow One Course Until Successful)

By

Lindsay Hopkins

ISBN-13: 978-1478220053

ISBN-10:1478220058

Legal Disclaimers & Notices

This book is presented to you for informational purposes only and is not a substitute for any professional advice. The contents herein are based on the views and opinions of the author and all associated contributors.

While every effort has been made by the author and all associated contributors to present accurate and up to date information within this document, it is apparent that technologies and philosophies rapidly change. Therefore, the author and all associated contributors reserve the right to update the contents and information provided herein as these changes progress. The author and/or all associated contributors take no responsibility for any errors or omissions if such discrepancies exist within this document.

The author and all other contributors accept no responsibility for any consequential actions taken, whether monetary, legal, or otherwise, by any and all readers of the materials provided. It is the reader's sole responsibility to seek professional advice before taking any action on their part.

Readers' results will vary based on their skill level and individual perception of the contents herein, and thus no guarantees, monetarily or otherwise, can be made accurately. Therefore, no guarantees are made.

Lindsay Hopkins

CONTENTS

About the Author   7

Testimonials   14

Foreword   15

How to use this book   19

Why I wrote this book   21

Acknowledgements   22

My Journey   24

10 Key Learning Points   30

Chapter 1 – Understand How You Work   35

Chapter 2 – The Three 'C's'   52

Chapter 3 – Positive and Negative Beliefs   70

Chapter 4 – Green Dragons vs White Knights   89

Chapter 5 – Positive Affirmations   103

Chapter 6 – Goals, Intentions, Dreams   115

Chapter 7 – Grab Back Your Life   130

Conclusion   145

What Next?   146

Recommended Reading and References   152

Lindsay Hopkins

About the Author

I was born in Amersham (Buckinghamshire, England) on the 15th November 1958 into an Army family (mum and dad were both from South Wales). My father had done National Service in the Welsh Fusiliers and then taken a commission in the Royal Army Education Corps, mum had been a WREN and was also a trained opera singer. My first real memory as a child was running wild and free in Nakuru, Kenya whilst dad served with the Kings African Rifles, a joyous 3-4 years, a time of space, beautiful countryside, adventures, play and laughter. A brief spell back in Strensall in Yorkshire and then off to even more adventures in Singapore for 3 years (another great army posting for mum and dad). 3 years of heat (which I loved) excitement, smells of the orient, colours and the charm of the Far East.

At the age of 11 I went off to boarding school at the Duke of York's Royal Military School in Dover with about 500 other boys. It was a rugby, cricket, swimming, cross-country running army school, for army orphans and sons of serving soldiers. Some people hate boarding school,(like both my sister and my brother), but in truth, barring one short 6 week patch at the age of 14, when my father rescued me for an exeat (half day out) and talked me through my "homesick pain" I embraced boarding school life. I loved the sport, the friends and once the regime was understood I knew exactly how to have fun and woke up every day (or most days anyway) with a massive smile on my face. I am lucky I have always had my default mood as that of 100% happiness! I studied hard (we had no choice), swam for the school, played rugby for the school all the way up to the 1st XV and became the Head of School in my last year. A model student, but not a perfect one - I had many a caning and detention on my way through the school I can assure you!

I applied for 5 universities, Liverpool was my first choice and Oxford and Cambridge were my 4th and 5th choices, which didn't go down well with my tutors. I was given what was known as an unconditional place at Liverpool to study Marine Zoology (I fancied being the second Jacques Cousteau). In my final term at school my headmaster grabbed me into his study and asked me if I fancied "having a bash" at the Royal Commissions Board (RCB) selection at Westbury to become sponsored through the army at University. I really had no desire to become an army officer but the idea of being paid whilst I was at University was to me a great one. I passed the RCB first time, much to my amazement.

Liverpool University at the age of 18, after a brief spell at Sandhurst, (Camberley), on what was known as the "one pip wonder course", was total bliss. Great friendships were forged, lots of rugby, lots of parties, lots of relationships and even some lectures. I swapped from Marine Zoology to Psychology after attending a psychology lecture as a guest and I simply fell in love with the subject. I really felt it was far more me. I finally emerged with a very average 2:2 BSc with Honours.

During university I grabbed the chance to go back to my Regiment (the 1st Royal Tank Regiment) whenever I could but also had some great adventures which included 3 "amigos" busking around Europe on Euro Rail. Learning how to be a Mountain Leader in the Highlands of Scotland and learning how to ski for a month in Bavaria with the army.

Following my Graduation I went back to Sandhurst for the full-on course to learn how to be an Army Officer. I made more superb friends and almost without exception had a glorious time there for 6 months. I have no doubt the school experience and military regime helped my mindset. I think the only exception was on the final exercise in South Wales on the Brecon Beacons at 2.00 a.m in a bleak January when I truly questioned the wisdom of guarding a trench against four sheep whilst the snow fell upon my head. I could not see the benefit of frost bite and hyperthermia while sitting in my own homeland! Luckily the Guards Colour Sergeant who looked after our platoon as an instructor, made me see sense with several slugs of port from his hip flask and some very firm sage words of wisdom. I passed the course and "graduated" again on the main square of Sandhurst, sword in hand, watched by my proud parents and my fiancée to be Chrissy, (who I had met whilst on leave over the Christmas period).

I learned the mastery of becoming a tank Commander at Lulworth and Bovington camp in Dorset for a further 6 months, together with 30 other armoured corps young officers, but this time the fun was being treated as a semi grown up for the first time. Now we had our commissions and soldiers even had to call us "sir" and salute us (even if they didn't mean it!). Following Dorset I returned to Germany to **where the Regiment was based - at that time each Regiment in the British Army was about 400/500 men and 60/70 tanks -** to a life of fun but relative calm as, luckily for me, there was no real action going on in the world apart from the troubles in Northern Ireland which the Regiment did get involved with.

I loved my short time in the army and I made some truly superb friends which have endured through my whole life. But sadly I suffered some form of breakdown and spent 2-3 months in Woolwich Military Hospital where they tried to work out what was wrong with me! I was not well at all and had all the tests you can imagine to fathom why I had "gone off the rails". At one point I was even being challenged for fabricating the "condition" to get out of repaying my University fees and not serving the rest of my army contract. But 4 Army Medical Boards soon cleared that concern up, thanks to the support from my father, who was by that time a Colonel. To this day it is not clear what happened. I guess we could call it Post Traumatic Stress Disorder. But to be honest, I have never been inclined to go back and revisit this section of my life. What happened, happened. A tough time I must confess.

The Army Medical Board deemed me unfit for further service in a "teeth arm", (as in front-line soldiering) and so I was given the choice of the Army Pay Corps, The Army Catering Corps or a gratuity and an honourable exit after a set period of continued service. I chose to leave. I did however have 9-12 months still to serve. So I was sent up to work with the great explorer Colonel Blashford Snell, (of Operation Raleigh and Drake fame), up in Fort George, Inverness with the Fort George Volunteers teaching young inner city children how to embrace the highlands.

During this time I had leave to finally marry Chrissy after a cancellation due to illness. We were "granted" a few days leave in London by the army, but our main honeymoon was touring the highlands in the guise of conducting a reconnaissance for the following year's Fort George Volunteers in a VW Golf GTI, all expenses paid! It emerged after our two week break that no reconnaissance report was actually required.

I returned for the last time to my Regiment at Bovington Camp with Chrissy to commence my 'gardening leave', where you were allowed as much time off as you needed to hunt for jobs outside the army. I applied to every FTSE 100 company I could find with an impeccable CV but the mental aberration or medical "blip" prevented any job offers heading my way. My conclusion was that the only way forward was a commission-only role in a Financial Services Company in London. "No training required". I applied and was accepted, (surprise surprise!!). So off I went to London town "where the streets are paved with gold".

I must say that I swapped a khaki uniform or rather black tank coveralls really, for the new City Uniform - a pin-striped suit, white shirt and silk tie, with ease. I was so excited, we were "motivated" every day by our enthusiastic managers who were taught to lead by example and so enthusiasm was very high every single day. It was a 'lead from the front', 'total commitment', 'judge by results' environment. The work ethos of 'in early, leave late' and a recognition system was enough to stimulate even a dormant polar bear. I loved it - the challenges, the comradeship, the ups and downs and the learning, plus, quite simply, being in "The City'. I worked for 9 superb years in the Porchester Group, which then morphed into the MI Group and finally City Financial. I rose from Trainee Consultant to Branch Manager in 18 months and then started to build a team of sales people who worked under me for over-ride commission. The team size increased from 0 to about 40 in a two-year period. I think I ended up as a Senior Branch Manager and so from recruit, (I was recruit number 97), the company grew to 3,000-plus strong nationwide.

Luckily I stayed ahead of the pack and was one of the top 10 managers. I won loads of conventions as all the good people did which entailed 5-star trips with your partner once a year all round the world, San Francisco, Los Angeles, Hawaii, all round the Caribbean, Singapore, Bali, Australia and many more far flung destinations. But sadly when the original CEO and gladiator left us under a cloud my heart left the business too. A hard wrench for me as loyalty was one of our USP's, but the love of the role left me.

I was head-hunted into the infamous Allied Dunbar with lots of promises and a large cheque, as long as I brought my team with me which I did in the main in a "top secret" operation over one Easter Holiday. I was blanked by all my friends who I left behind but I was sure it was the right move for me. I adored the six courses of one to two week management training we had to do down in the residential training centre in Swindon and I loved the learning. We were taught all the aspects of business management, coaching styles, interview techniques and selection methods. I quite simply lapped all this information up and applied it within my daily running of the Branch in Haymarket (near Trafalgar Square).

I was becoming fed up with managing and coaching sales people who were earning more than me. It seemed like far more fun to actually run a practice and get out there selling to clients and be able to build a practice that actually had a value to sell after a few years. So with permission from my senior director I emerged over the course of a year from being a manager to setting up my own practice, Trafalgar Square Financial Planning Consultants (within Allied Dunbar), with a small team. I did well and enjoyed more conventions, awards and accolades.

At the time though there was only one place to work if you were fully qualified and a reasonable salesperson/adviser, which I had become, and that was The Rothschild Partnership and they had been chatting with me for some years. I moved with a nice joining fee, (a bit like a footballer), and enjoyed a further two years in what then became known as the St James Place Partnership. I must mention this was not without a High Court case raised against me by Allied Dunbar which was beaten off soundly! At Rothschild we were dealing with wealth management and high net worth individuals with a tremendous focus on customer care, service and spending time with clients, which I loved. It was less about the numbers through the door, and more about building up long-term relationships. It was great fun, great learning and very, very civilized, and just around the corner from the Bank of England in the heart of the City.

In the Autumn of 2002 one or two things were bugging me and despite the scare tactics of the big companies telling us that it's cold out there if we go out on our own, I simply needed to find out if this was true. My sales figures were dropping but my own mortgage business, which I was allowed to run in conjunction with being a partner in St James, was going O.K. I parted company in a civilized and amicable way unlike my two previous very frosty experiences.

So there I was on the 23rd December 2002 with a new business to start and a garden shed! So that's where Trafalgar Square Financial Planning Consultants really started. Whilst initially I could only advise on mortgages, I moved into the full Independent Financial Adviser role some time later. I had one aim and that was to be my own boss and earn a healthy six figures to support my family. That worked year one and with the help of two tremendously loyal people in my team, and some very good support from friends and family, things took shape beautifully.

From 2003 to 2007 turnover doubled every year and the company size grew from 3 to nigh on 27. I worked tirelessly but had great fun and during 2003-2006 built a business to business company called Trafalgar Square Solutions which packaged mortgages for other brokers, an Overseas Mortgage Company called Trafalgar Square Overseas and offshore investment company Trafalgar Square Investments which focussed on offshore property funds. Life was good, busy, profitable and of course, varied.

There was synergy between all the companies and so the multi-company concept was not terrifying, and I had a very solid team to support everything, and the infrastructure was there. I was very lucky to work with some great people. Around 2006 I also set up a bridging finance company with a business partner, (the first ever Secret Millionaire, Gill Fielding), called Secure the Bridge.

Way back in 2003/2004 I had been invited by an old client of mine from Rothschild days to be a guest speaker/trainer with a property education company and so I became a regular speaker with Whitney UK, (this company is to-day known as Tigrent). The training appearances increased over the years to the point where for at least 5-6 weekends a year I was on my feet co–presenting a course known as Creative Finance for upwards of 50–60 individuals at a time.

This exposure and experience initiated requests from individuals for a little more than financial advice, more on coaching concepts which suited me down to the ground as this was at the heart of what I really wanted to do. The Creative Finance course became more and more personal development centred from my point of view and so the coaching side of things simply evolved naturally. The financial services world was always very pro-positive mind-set and so from that point on in my life I engaged a coach once a month to help me move forward.

Weaved in amongst all this I had been asked to become a parent Governor at Swaffield Primary school where my son had been at school, and after 3 years became appointed as Chair of Governors, a position I still hold - in fact I am now into my 11th year as chair! Plus I joined the Association of International Property Professionals due to my link with Overseas Mortgages. I joined the board and subsequently became elected chairman of this board for 2 enjoyable years. Not easy running a board of 18 feisty overseas property entrepreneurs I can tell you, but it yielded invaluable business experience and great contacts.

I think many books have been written about what happened to the economy between 2008 and 2010 but needless to say it was carnage and the financial services aspects of my businesses, particularly mortgages, saw bloodshed and mayhem with a 70% downturn in turnover literally overnight! No one was left un-scathed and whilst I had seen recessions I had never been a business owner during one of these events before. We had many casualties and no one escaped un-scarred. We held on to the life boats and kept rowing! I lost some businesses, and sadly lost some friendships, but everyone was fighting for their lives. I certainly don't hold any grudges and I hope none are harboured against me. I have always had good friends around me, and good support from my family, and so we resolved not to throw the towel in. But thank goodness I had decided to diversify.

To-day

I live with my wife and two children in London. I am involved in loads of things and I guess the easiest way to describe my professional world today is that it's divided up into two sectors - Finance and Coaching/Training. Most of my business activities involve two or more partners to "pool" skills, and my principle of multiple income streams still holds fast.

My Current Businesses Activities

1.Trafalgar Square Financial Planning Consultants (TSFPC) (www.trafalgarsq.co.uk) holds strong and whilst somewhat shrunken in size since 2007. It still retains the position as one of the niche suppliers of buy-to-let mortgages in the UK. It remains in a healthy position.

2. Trafalgar Square Overseas Ltd (www.trafalgarsqoverseas.co.uk) is an overseas mortgage business which is alive and kicking and now specializes more in building and launching small niche, alternative and unregulated collective investments.

3. Secure the Bridge (www.securethebridge.com) is a short term bridging finance company which services in the main the clients of TSFPC, focussing on the buy-to-let market and this has been going from strength to strength over the last few years.

Coaching/Training

1. Future Performance Coaching (www.futureperfomancecoaching.com) is a private coaching business for my own clients which has been operating since 2007 and grows from strength to strength.

2.The T60 Coaching Programme (www.t60coaching.com) is currently a specialist high-intensity coaching programme offered exclusively to Tigrent clients, provided by a team of specialist coaches which I co-ordinate, with a partner, focussing on property and business.

3. Millionaire Action Plans (M.A.P.s) is a membership mastermind business and property support group involving aspiring entrepreneurs who want to get going quickly with the right sort of grass roots support.

I run private seminars/workshops through the year and still present as a speaker with many of the courses with Tigrent each year. I am on the UK

Property Network circuit as a keynote speaker and I like to be 'on my feet' for one of these events at least once a month.

Life is busy, fruitful and rewarding and it allows me to have multiple income streams, a platform for creativity and the continuity to 'step up' and F.O.C.U.S. (Follow One Course Until Successful).

Testimonials

"Lindsay is one of life's gentlemen. Highly personable and of the utmost integrity he blends deep and broad knowledge of his core financial services business with a natural gift and passion for teaching and mentoring others."

Bradley Wright

"I have had the pleasure of knowing Lindsay for many years. He is always fun, honest and hard working. His degree of enthusiasm is unsurpassable and his knowledge and empathy is deep rooted. He has a manner that is supportive yet guiding and constructive and his level of knowledge is amazing. If you have not met him, you should do!"

Annie Davidson

"Lindsay is an amazing coach especially in helping one to succeed quickly in reaching one's goals. He cares deeply and is committed to one's success. Lindsay is a very positive person who encourages you to be solution-orientated and look at issues in a different way. I highly recommend Lindsay as a performance coach."

Marie Sheehan

"Lindsay does not pull any punches and gets right to both the point and the heart of the matter. I found him to be a great encourager and a person who can spot what it is that motivates someone to reach inside, grasp the potential that is there, believe in it and then make it happen."

Carol Lee

Foreword

By Steve Smith

I first met Lindsay Hopkins In 1977 at Liverpool University, he was part of the same "crazy gang" which emanated from Roscoe and Gladstone Hall. Even in those early days Lindsay struck me as an energetic, creative and positive person. He always had more money than the rest of us; and it wasn't long before we discovered that he was in the Army and when he disappeared off on weekends it wasn't to have a holiday but to drive tanks. Our paths interwove over the weeks and months that followed. We both played sport for the University: Lindsay rugby and me, golf. I believe Lindsay was asked to leave his Hall of Residence relatively early for some misdemeanour, (turning the swans in Roscoe and Gladstone hall lake purple with Potassium Permanganate), and so he found a superb flat in the famous Liverpool 8 postcode. In the second year he persuaded four of his mates to join him and that became our base of operations for the next two years. Lindsay and our good friend Tim Forster played guitar and performed together regularly at halls of residence and a variety of bars including the Everyman Theatre. How he struck me then? Creative, good fun, a loyal friend and full of a lust for life which left most individuals standing.

After University we went our separate ways for a few years. A couple of years later I heard that Lindsay had left the Army and got married! He was coming up to London to work in the City and very soon our paths crossed again. Lindsay was in sales and as a friend I did everything I could to help him move forward. He was driven, motivated and sincere in his pursuit of targets but not to the disadvantage of his clients. He was insistent on "spending time with his clients" in very long lunches and huge great swathes of social adventures; he was good at both 1:1 interactions and equally loved to be a party animal.

There was a time when I broke up with my first wife and needed a place to stay while I took a deep breath and the offer of a bed came without question despite our busy lives - Lindsay, Chrissy and me! I borrowed the odd shirt and tie, one of which I never gave back and still wear! How did he strike me then? Motivated, a loyal friend, caring towards other people, loving to his new family and still a man with an inspiring passion for life, laughter and fun.

As the years progressed I remained a client of Lindsay's in a variety of investment deals etc. But he and I knew one key element of the relationship was our quarterly lunch where we invariably re-invented ourselves whilst putting the world to rights! The years passed and I saw Lindsay build up a sales team who seemed to worship the ground he walked on. I saw him achieve accolade after accolade for 'top sales this' and 'top sales that' and disappear off on 5-star conventions all round the world, (I called them jollies), every year from the age of about 27 all the way through to early 40's. I was however aware of his financial stresses not least the destruction, (not by Lindsay), of his valuable share options at the Porchester Group. This had devastating results which took Lindsay years to recover from. I was aware that there was a groundswell of unhappiness seeping into his life as he moved from Allied Dunbar to the Rothschild Partnership, (laterally known as the St James Place Partnership). I sensed that his time of being a cog in the wheel was coming to an end. How did he strike me then? A professional sales manager, a motivator of people, a caring leader, a creative manager and a great value-based sales person.

It was December 2002 when he resigned from the St James's Place partnership and January 2003, (aged 44), when he took the brave step to set up on his own from his garden shed. I must confess to have admired this bold step. From a healthy 6 figure income to the world of the unknown was a step most people would not take; especially when there were school fees and a not insignificant Wandsworth mortgage to consider! But Lindsay dived into building TSFPC with such passion it wasn't very long before he announced that he had 3 staff and new offices and this story kept a momentum which was incredible, doubling his turnover every year and reaching a team size of 27+.

I know he was leading his business with all the lessons he had learned over the years and clearly the point he reached in January 2003 was a "tipping point "in his life. The quest to own something yourself, the quest for responsibility, the ability to create one's own world. How did he strike me then? Passionate, committed to success, sharing with his team, a man with a vision.

From then on Lindsay kept on building businesses, never huge ones, but healthy ones. He started speaking at a variety of Property Training Courses and his confidence in this arena grew and grew. We went into business together at one point in 2005/2008 building an Offshore Property Fund. That was a great time and the mix of friendship and business was great fun. The issues of the 2007/2008 downturn hit Lindsay hard and his Trafalgar Team reduced significantly but what emerged in parallel, almost as if planned was a training, coaching, speaking business spread across 3 brands which meant that Lindsay seemingly weathered the storm through 2008–2010/11 with ease, but one thing was different. His true passion for helping people, (he calls it mentoring and coaching), was emerging. It is sometimes strange to see how, after years and years of pursuing a particular career, that someone finds the true path they wish to follow. How did he strike me then? A little battered by the credit crunch to be fair, but resilient, creative and unprepared to accept that his goals should be compromised.

Now Lindsay and I are lifelong friends and when I was asked to write the foreword for this book I was very honoured. I am an avid reader of everything. I do believe knowledge is power. Lindsay's world of coaching, positive motivation and helping people is not the same as mine but I respect his total commitment to share and help people move forward.

I can see what he is doing in this book, he is touching upon elements that have helped him move forward and enjoy the *journey* rather than enjoy the *end result*. He is completely open about his trials and tribulations and yet as a successful businessman and coach he has a modesty which is extraordinary. I know you will enjoy this read. I also know there is so much more to come from Lindsay and so over the next few years I suspect this will not be the only Foreword I write. Enjoy the book. The creative format is superb, very Lindsay, and I would say the same as Lindsay; please take at least one nugget from the book - be it a success habit to adopt or the seed of an idea to help you achieve your goals.

By Gill Fielding, 'Secret Millionaire'

I first met Lindsay at a presentation when he walked up to the front of the room at a training weekend in Edgware Road, London. He dropped all his overhead view foils on the way up, (luckily), didn't bother to pick them up and then gave an intuitive, funny, balanced presentation for an hour to 60 property students and was a "wow"! I shudder to think what it would have been like if he had actually followed his script. Lindsay doesn't work that way! Some of us rehearse whereas he is often best caught on the hop.

Some years later and I have now sat with Lindsay in many meetings and presentations and I have begun to realise that the preparation and notes are all in his head, having been drilled there from countless hours of rehearsal and development. Every time I go into Lindsay's office I am like a child in a sweet shop looking at all his personal development DVDs, books and materials – I have never known a man so engrossed in, and passionate about, personal development, the search for excellence and self-awareness.

This manifests itself in a variety of guises: I particularly like his ability with time management making sure that he uses every second of every day in the best way possible, and in his case it's the early morning hours that work best. Lindsay constantly strives towards better and greater achievements for himself and those connected with him and I find his relentless pursuit of excellence both impressive and inspirational.

He has some great success habits – another one I admire is the 'rudder for the day' as Lindsay knows that if you start off the day with the wrong thinking and the wrong attitude, it steers the day off on the wrong course – and every day on the wrong course is one day out of one life wasted.

Lindsay's point of difference as a human being is the ability to keep going with those success habits every day, week, month and year, which he achieves by a forward focus on the future combined with brilliant goal setting, review and enhancing affirmations.

As a man Lindsay is great company, fun and caring: brilliant with money and financial planning whether that be global strategic finance or the smaller money matters. He is always upbeat, always honorable and always a loyal friend.

This book will encourage to you to develop the habits that make Lindsay the exceptional person he is ... I urge you to use this brilliant book to achieve the same level of excellence for yourself.

How to use this book

It is a little bit of an insult, as you are more than capable of reading a book! So perhaps what I really mean is what were my thoughts as to the layout and how to use the book most effectively.

↻ So in the top corner of every page is a quote that has further inspired me, jolted me forward or tickled my fancy. I have always enjoyed quotes and they often make me quite literally stop in my tracks and have a think.

I tend to see them not as show stoppers but as show starters, a jump-start for a sleepy brain. You have choices, we all do, it's your book. So go in and out of the quotes as you wish. Use them as a kick-start to reading each page. Or flick through them randomly as an energiser when you want to pull out a quote for your writing, a speech, a presentation or maybe to put on your wall or your fridge.

⮑ I think the main text is self-explanatory and you can, I hope, take joy in flicking through the book from start to finish just like you would do with a normal book. You can ignore all the rest of the whacky sections if you wish!

↻ The affirmations section runs through the whole book and it is a central theme to this book, my life and my coaching. You will read in the book how strongly I believe in these affirmations to mount a continuous program of positive input into our brains to counter the continuous bombardment of negativity hitting us every day. Dip in an out of these affirmations as you wish.

⮑ Each chapter has a story running through the base of each page. Why? Well it is a little bit of a message. The power of metaphor to make a point is a renowned tool used by coaches, speakers, leaders and politicians the world over. It is not meant to distract you or divert you from the main text. You can read it in parallel with the main text or simply digest it all in one go.

☭ Notes are notes of course! But for me taking ownership of a book with post-it notes, highlighter pens or side notes is the key to what I have done for many, many years. Helping to jolt me into active reading, deciding to actually use some of the pointers, advice or guidelines actually in my life, to change things, create momentum, and add power to my journey.

Each chapter has a 'mind map' to summarise the chapter. I used these to plan the writing of the book but what I have done is only include a digital version so that you have a translation from my awful handwriting!

At the end I show a mind map of one of the books I have read to show you how I summarise what I have learnt. This might be something that you could do, at the end of this book, for yourself.

Why I wrote this Book

Since 2003 I have privately coached in excess of 300 individuals and couples in the areas of personal development, business start-up, business growth and also in the area of property portfolio building.

In addition to this, in conjunction with my business partner Mark Dalton, and a group of fellow specialist coaches we have now finished in excess of 100 sixty-day coaching programs under contract from Tigrent Learning (UK).

During this time I have seen triggers that help people reach 'Eureka!' moments where they have made a significant break-through in their life journey.

I have also identified and tested a whole series of personal strategies and tactics for people to apply and weave into their lives to speed up their journey, reduce some pain and oil the wheels towards consistent goal completion.

This book is intended to reach out and help even more people gain purpose, self-confidence and to be able to 'step up' and F.O.C.U.S. - Follow One Course Until Successful (Robert Kiyosaki).

Acknowledgements

I have as yet never won a BAFTA or a BRIT award and I am not goal-orientated to do so. But unlike a lot of people I do like it when individuals receive their awards and take time to thank people who have helped them on their journey and I would like to do the same.

I have thought long and hard on this and I decided that the most politically balanced way to do this was to thank as many people as I can simply using one sentence for each. One thing is for sure, if I have missed you out it is done without malice and if you have shared my journey to date you are bound to have made a contribution and I thank you.

I would like to thank:-

- My wife Chrissy for her love, belief and total patience over the last 30 plus years.

- My daughter Gabby and my son Daniel for their love respect and the laughter they have brought into my life.

- My dog Ollie for listening to my morning affirmations and pretending to understand them.

- My mother for ensuring that every moment of my life up the age of 18 was an absolute adventure.

- My father for my 9.00 a.m Saturday briefings which I love and adore.

- My sister Belinda for her total love, support and inspiration to put pen to paper.

- My brother Jon who makes me smile whenever he writes or says anything to me.

- My loyal friend and godfather to my daughter Timothy John Orchard who has helped me out of more scrapes than I can remember.

- My Trafalgar Square Business partner from the outset Sarah Jane Costello and her very creative husband Richard for their help and absolute loyalty at all times.

- My personal assistant for more years than I can remember Jeannie Woollen for patience, support, loyalty and friendship beyond the call of duty.

- To every member of any company I have worked with and set up past and present. I know we have had fun.

- To my coaches over the years Stuart Goodship, Colin Clark, Nick Williams and latterly Pam Richardson.

- To my business partner Gill Fielding (Secure Bridge) for belief, support and trust.

- To my business partner Mark Dalton for helping me 'step up' to the plate and get on with it.

- To all the beautiful humans with whom I work in M.A.P.s, the T60 programme, (as coaches and clients), and Tigrent Learning (UK).

- To Iain Edwards, (CEO Tigrent UK), for one simple conversation many years ago which changed my world.

- To my private JV partner Sean Thompson who offers me fun, friendship and adventure on a regular basis.

- To my closest friend in the whole world Steven Smith who has believed in me since I was 18 and made me laugh ever since.

- To my dear deceased friend Jim Hawkins who knows I hung around after he went to heaven as I had "things left to do".

- To Sue Searle for guiding and cajoling me to put this book together despite its complex format, and for contributing some of the affirmations from her book *Affirmations for Success*. Also to Mindgenius.com for helping me with the mind maps at the end of each chapter.

- I must also thank the Carluccio's chain of restaurants, and particularly the branch in Putney by the river, where I have written many a word of this book looking out over the Thames.

My Journey

Somebody the other day said to me "Yeah! But it's easy for you!" Well, interestingly enough one of my coaches, Nick Williams, asked me to complete the exercise that follows to remind me of my journey since the age of 23 and then give that young man some advice knowing what I know now.

So here are these two exercises:-

This is how I got where I am:	Skills learnt:
In February 1982 my entire world which I had spent much time planning was smashed to pieces when I awoke in my army hospital bed, wired up to numerous machines and drugged up to my eyeballs on a vicious cocktail of scary drugs. My pride and confidence, once so evident at the Sandhurst passing out parade just a year earlier had completely disappeared. I spent 3 months in Woolwich Military Hospital.	Accept support from friends and family
A year later I swapped one uniform for another – my black tank regiment coveralls for a pin-striped suit. It felt very strange as I went off to join the world of financial services 'hard selling' in the City.	Resilience – overcome the fear
I was given the company training manual, (a copy of the Yellow Pages), and told that by the time I had made 60 calls, spoken to 40 people, and made 5 appointments every day for 3 months my training would be complete.	Persistence Handling rejection
I learned all about the 'numbers game', targeting, presentation, how to relate to people quickly and the 'dark art' of handling objection and rejection.	Sales ratios Activity regimes Objection handling
I established a work ethic second to none today. 'when you are there be there. Don't mess around, full-on focus, work to a daily target, push yourself to the	Time planning

maximum and have fun!'	
Over the next 9 months I climbed the commission-only ladder of hierarchy and then took on my own team.	Target planning Realism vs Optimism
I replaced blackmail management and manipulation, (which was a method used by other managers of teasing and bullying to get results), with care management and motivation. I built a team of 40 advisors who were happy, supported and earning money.	Being open to new opportunities Team building
Motivation by commitment, (overspending), was the self induced legacy with which I left the MI Group, but I took a whole lot more too – a growing confidence, an understanding of 'realistic' target setting and competition. Above all I had learned the ability to be motivated and to motivate others to achieve a Herculean sales target despite all odds; an 'irrespective success' template for the future.	Financial management Stress management "Sharpen the Saw"
Eminently recruitable, I was headhunted along with my whole team, (35 of whom came with me), to the then infamous Allied Dunbar where I ran my 'Trafalgar Square' branch with a sense of professionalism, (the AD hard sell days were now all but gone).	Coaching Recruitment Appraisals
I attended and enjoyed 6 one week residential management training courses in Swindon which gave me superb knowledge in selection processes, coaching, compliance and different styles of management. The luxury sales conventions allowed me to see the world in a privileged way. Paris, Bali, Singapore, Hawaii, Sydney, Great Barrier Reef, San Francisco, Key West, LA, Barbados, St Lucia, Martinique, Grand Cayman, Cape town, and 2 5 star luxury cruises.	Performance management Financial regulation Sales styles Personality Styles
In the world of financial services the grass is always greener, so it was the lure of a big fat cheque (£50,000), that made me skip off to join the re-named	Goal Setting Self

St James's Place in 1998. High court - Lindsay Hopkins vs Allied Dunbar.	Discipline
Unfortunately the MI Group legacy of "spend it then earn it" was still with me and my personal debts had crept up to circa £90k.	Focus, determination stamina and tenacity "Bottle"
The continuous juggling and 'robbing of Peter to pay Paul' was mentally draining but I had declared all to my new company and through them I learned the value of a 'high profile' brand, positioning myself with clients as a genuine adviser, portfolio management and a superb selection of presentation styles. The management support was genuine, caring and mature in a market where manipulation was still the hallmark.	Vision Positive Mental Attitude Determin-ation
I thrived for the first year and achieved partner status quickly, meaning I prospected, (found), 100 new clients, averaged £12K per month personally and introduced £4.5 million of investment into the company. But one can only run so fast and eventually the wolves caught up with me. The mental stresses of dealing daily with debt forced me to take out an Individual Voluntary Arrangement (the closest one can get to bankruptcy). St James's Place Partnership supported me to a point until the higher echelons became unhappy, and, on the 23rd December 2002 I returned home from the city having resigned, (my choice!).	Recommend-ation Selling Financial structuring
I had started Trafalgar Square Financial Planning 2 years earlier running it on a parallel basis with SJP, so in January 2003 I moved into my garden shed and started marketing like crazy. I was scared, but also motivated, inspired and driven. I entered into the world of seminar speaking doing a	Marketing Business Start-Ups Belief in Oneself

regular guest spot for a property education company (Whitney) and soon the phones were ringing off the hook. For the last 5 years life has been a roller coaster ride of excitement and creation. I've been like a kid in a sweetshop, finding businesses with a synergy to mine and building businesses to my own template.	Networking Public Speaking Business Confidence
Moving from sole trader to managing director of several companies (most of which I own), I have built my own personal regime of daily, weekly and monthly 'habits' which I do not veer from. These form my 'handrails of success'. Making money helps too!	Business Models Strategies Success Habits

Advice I would give to Lindsay Hopkins (aged 23):-

There are a series of stages involved in creating a good life and within each stage there is a series of processes. Some people master these stages and processes very quickly, some never master them at all. What I would like to do is help you understand the stages and processes needed to create your good life. Once established, the pace at which you progress is of course up to you. But, I can assure you a joyous life is one with clear direction. It is far more fun driving when you know where you are going, the vehicle is fast, the road is clear and the mist lifted!

Stage One – self appreciation/understanding

Stage Two – appreciating others

Stage One

'Know thyself' is, I believe, a quote from Socrates – but what great advice from a great man. The key to almost anything in life is to understand who you are, your beliefs, values, skills, strengths and weaknesses and aspirations for the future. This understanding by the way, is an ever changing picture but it is imperative that, like taking a passport photograph of yourself each year of your life and putting it into a photo album, you take stock to see who you are, what you look like and what you are looking for.

There are numerous ways to take the steps and apply the processes required in Stage One. Obviously the earlier and younger you define your life mission, your value system and skills you have, the better. Using any number of methods to achieve this 'self audit' will put you in a position to start planning your map of the future, (your goals). Why? Let's face it, you would always use a road map to get to somewhere you don't know, so why risk taking a chance on your life?

One way to create your life plan and then stick to it is to establish a series of disciplines or what I prefer to call 'hand rails of success'. This is the code you live by, knowing that you are ultimately always giving yourself the best possible spring board to achieve your aims in life, be they personal or business.

The hand rails of success I use are a series of annual, monthly, weekly and daily habits which, if you establish them as part of 'what you do', just like breathing, they will become your allies as you move towards success.

Stage Two

We are seldom on stage alone and we must therefore learn to understand the other actors. What I mean by that is that as we are set to succeed we must learn to interact with other human beings in an effective way. We set out to gain progress and win our way to achieving our goals with the help of other people in a mutually winning way. 'Give and you shall receive' is great line from the Bible. This is a truism that cannot be challenged.

We must initiate a learning path concerned with human beings, so that our understanding of them grows as we grow. The most powerful human interaction tool I have ever mastered is the understanding of personality types which allows us to communicate with people in the way they want to be communicated with. This is a hard discipline to master but the difference it makes when you work with understanding compared to the "I'll do it my way" is astounding.

The personality styles are linked to understanding the basics of what makes us 'tick', be it the use and understanding of the hierarchy of human needs, (Maslow), or Dilt's neurological levels of change. There is a philosophy which says that we can then interact with people as 'masters'. Be careful though, this 'mastering' is with the aim of human management not manipulation which is another fundamental decision we have to make. We match our actions and words to the people we are dealing with and what they want to achieve, because what we want to achieve, is mutual benefit.

Conclusion

These two stages are not easy and they will take time to develop but you will see the fruits of your labour quicker than you could ever imagine. You will make thousands of mistakes along the way but that is how you will learn, if you don't make mistakes you are not progressing and so every error is a sign of reassurance that you are moving forward.

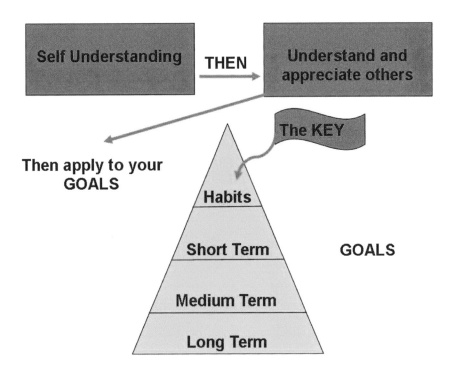

The 10 Key Learning Points which have been 'My Success Habits' to date

'Zig Zag Your Way to Success'

This metaphor is borne from the need to take your time when climbing up a mountain rather than trying to run straight to the top. The same is very true of achieving goals. I have used these 10 steps to share with individuals during my network meeting talks over the years. These are quite simply success habits which I have adopted and placed into my life to keep me moving in the right direction. These are not goals, these are elements of behaviour which have been adopted as a norm to help me constantly move forward.

1. Understand the value of time:
Every DAY counts / Every HOUR counts

It's a chilling thought but if you reflect back on yesterday, its already gone. It will not come back and you have either used it or abused it. If you wish to craft a good life then you must value every day and every week; it's not good enough to say 'oh I am having a bad day today' or 'well, this week is not going well'.

I admit we cannot craft every minute of our time but even if we can chunk it down to half days and be aware of what is going on then at least if it's going badly or not effectively we can change its direction. Take a break. Take stock and think on what you need to do in order to turn the day around. Is this over analytical? Yes, I guess so but otherwise days slip into weeks which slip into months and you realise you've had a bad year. Goals slither down the plug hole and erode your self confidence. Each day should start with a 'hit list' of what you want to do.

2. Appreciate the 80/20 rule:
20% of your 'to Do List' will make you the most money or take you forward faster

Moving on to the hit list - every day should have a 'to do list'. It could be 10 things; it could be 100 things; if its 10 then 2 of the things on it will bring you the most benefit. If it's 100 things then 20 of them will reap the greatest rewards. It's hard work and it demands a great deal of effort. But, it's funny, because when I have a day with a 'to do list' compared with one without I get a lot more done.

Of course some days are better than others but if you commit to action and 'on purpose days' things will be better. I promise you. I do the 80/20 every week day and every weekend. At the weekend I simply change my focus to the family and lifestyle goals as opposed to work goals.

3. Learn to play to your strengths and to work with others who will cover your weaknesses:

Stop trying to be all things to all men/women. You are good at some things and not so good at others: the skill set of all the people I have met who are more successful than me is the art of maximising their strengths and asking other people to do the things that they don't like doing. This is not an admission of failure it is a genius step, because the people you work with like to do different things to you. Some like analysing, some like presenting, some like socialising, some like selling, some like organising. Why not tap into the strengths and skill sets of others? You are empowering them as well as getting them to help you!

4. Relish and maximise the days when you are 'On Form': Use them to move mountains because YOU CAN!

Some days you just can't help it; you are on form and flying! I guess scientists would call this biorhythms, others call it 'being in the flow', I call it a 'top of the form' day. Just go with the flow and maximise the day.

Try this: have a list of things you really can't handle:

The Brian Tracey 'frog' (this is a tough or hard task, one which you may have been dreading or one that you have been putting off for some time but you know it must be done) - some say if you have a frog to eat make it the first task of the day! But if it's a really horrid frog my advice might be to store it up for a 10/10 day when you feel like moving mountains; forging streams and jumping over oceans. You know these days happen, so use them don't abuse them!

5. Realise that with almost NO exception, everyone you ever meet can help you to succeed.

Everyone can and will help you at some stage in your life; so why don't you make that a fundamental decision? You will either work for them, with them or they will work for you. You will either sell to them, buy from them or they may sell for you. They may help you, you may help them or you might become partners. If you think about it the combinations are endless but if you have this mindset then the way you consider all the people you meet might well change. I am aware of how much I go on about TTP (Talk to People) and how it helps sales but if you match this mind set to anything you do it tends to change the way meeting people fits into your life. Of course you sometimes forget, but make it part of your inner self.

6. Identify that YOUR best 2 hours of the day should be when you need/want to do your best.

Just like our best day, we all have a best 2 hours of the day too. This is again a method which all 'top people' use! My best time is between 7am and 9am; that is when I create and think at my best. I guess if I could I would have all my key meetings at this time of the day and I certainly walk through life aware of this strength. How do you 'know' your best time? Simple, if you cannot tell, just spend one or two days taking stock each hour and grade yourself on a 1-10 scale.

10 = ace, 1 = bad. The message will come out loud and clear!

7. Understand that there is no joy in winning if the loser gets hurt: It MUST be a WIN / WIN.

Some humans trample their way to success and in my view live in a bad place! Evidence suggests that this is not the way forward. Win/win in **negotiation** is relatively easy but in fact it **can and should** apply to **everything**. In any given situation there can be a solution where all people can gain. The way to consider this from time to time is to step back before a confrontation, meeting or sale and think about the possible outcomes. Remember that the other person or persons involved may not have the same mindset, and of course the same value system as you, leaving them in a bad place. This must not stop you trying to get the best win/win outcome.

8. Work regularly on friendships: These must be nurtured and cherished as your most valuable assets.

I have recently done a life track exercise looking at where I was in primary school; secondary school; university and the army and then jobs from the age of 25 onwards. Looking back at who my friends were and whether I am still in touch. They are very important people who shared my life at that time. Having tracked my life the next step was to see how they are doing now. If they are doing better (relatively) than me then can they help me and of course vice versa. Either way I value the emotional investments I have made in my life and don't want to lose them. Try it! The worst that can happen is that you rekindle an old friendship over a beer.

9.Ensure that you work hard EVERY SINGLE DAY on BEING positive and SEEING positive in everything:

Being positive on a bad day is a real bummer. It takes strength, courage and damned hard work when you don't feel good; the world has dealt you a bad hand that day and all in all you just want the day to end. STOP IT. Take stock and see what you can do to change it! Ask your self what would the 'white knight' the positive guy/gal sitting on your shoulder do? Take a break and use a method I have found hard to master but have 90% time-managed to use to great affect: Take yourself out of the situation and have a 1-2 minute chat with the most important person in the arena **yourself!** Ask yourself how you are serving yourself by remaining in a negative state. Then ask yourself how you can change your state and how you can best serve this task.

10. ENJOY:
Smile as you travel the journey

I know a lot of you have seen poems and speeches about enjoying the journey. What this means is we do not and must not hold our breath and go through total pain and purgatory while we are moving through our lives and accomplishing our goals; that is not the game. We MUST make sure we are 'living' the journey along the way and enjoying it. Otherwise, to use the analogy of swimming a length underwater to get to the other end, it means that it is only when we get to the other end that we can take joy in the moment. We actually have to make sure that the journey is fun and fulfilling too. Sometimes this means we have to review and analyse our goals to make sure this is the case.

Chapter 1

"Understand How You Work"

A glimpse at:-

- Understanding yourself
- Learning styles
- Personality styles
- Neurolinguistic programming

All our dreams can come true if we have the courage to pursue them.

Walt Disney

NOTES:

Self-awareness is one of the keys to success, of that I am certain. I see it in all who succeed. At the same time, we all have our own journey and so success cannot be measured by comparison to anyone else, only by our own yardstick. I have often pondered about my own early years between the ages of 25 and 35. I do recall seeing many models of the world, of how people saw me, how I thought people considered me and how I thought about myself. I believe it is encapsulated in one study of the different versions of 'you' called the *Johari Window*. The suggestion here is that there are four ways that you exist or are seen by yourself and others.

- Known to others but not to me.

- Not known to me or known to others.

'Feel the fear, then do it anyway!'

Samuel

There was a young boy called Samuel who was brought up on a small Island near Bali where the population had remained low for some years. The island had all

- Known to me and others.

- Known to me but not to others.

Another way to look at is this:-

- How/who I am.

- How/who I think other people think I am.

- How/who other people actually think I am.

It really depends upon how brave you are, or indeed how determined you are to understand the way the world turns in your quest for reassurance. But it is essential in my mind for your progress to cross this bridge to learn to know who you are, how you work best and how you interface with people to greatest effect.

Once upon a time, about 5 years ago, I was with a mentor of mine, (I have always had a mentor or a coach to lean on. This is one of my key beliefs in life based upon all my reading. If you want to learn and grow always have a coach or a mentor to guide you and maintain accountability), and we were chatting in the board room at my offices. He actually temporarily lost his cool because I was talking about my own confidence and dealing with people. We had a Johari Window moment. The moment was very complimentary but also quite harsh. But I have never forgotten it.

> **The first principle of success is desire – knowing what you want. Desire is the planting of your seed.**
>
> *Robert Collier*

NOTES:

'I am working tirelessly to ensure that I live life with direction.'

---

modern necessities such as electricity and water but no TV, no broadband and no mobile phones. The culture on the island was simply to always help each other, to give constructive and honest feedback wherever possible and if

He said with furrowed brow and a rather angry tone "Lindsay, when will you actually reach the point of self-awareness and get with the programme? You are a gifted person and you have a charm and charisma which disarms people. You walk into any room, you smile and 99% of all mankind likes you. Now the key is to be aware of it, don't abuse this gift or factor in your personality. Don't abuse it. Simply recognise it. It allows you freedom to move around your world with confidence and so embrace this and stop faffing around! Embrace this to the betterment of other people. Get with the programme, you fool." See what I mean, harsh! Blunt, but one of the most honest compliments I have ever received.

I share this story with you and also with many clients who I work with and coach if they are backward in coming forward and they are walking in a shadow behind themselves. The key is to embrace and understand yourself. I share this story not to crow or be immodest I share this to help you realise that if one is self-aware one can also learn how to move forward towards success, happiness and fulfilment with so much more pace and certainty.

Ok how do we apply the Johari Window self-awareness methodology to move you forward? Well it's a brave move but you need to enlist the help of between 5 and 10 friends. In the first instance you simply jot down in let's say 6 sentences how you think you are as a person:-

> **The great thing in this world is not so much where we are, but in what direction we are moving**
>
> *Oliver Wendall Holmes*

NOTES:

'Where there is action, things change'

---

anything ever went wrong the focus was always on the positive and what learning can be taken from the bad event or experience. This applied to the islanders young and old.

1. I am considerate and caring.
2. I am good fun and amusing.
3. I am a good listener.
4. I am very creative.
5. I am a bit analytical.
6. I am popular.

You then consider in a different way, the way other people think of you:-

1. People think I am easy to get on with.
2. People think I am good socially.
3. People think I am friendly.
4. People think I am a deep thinker.
5. People think I am out-going.
6. People think I am caring.

You jot down what you think. Place this piece of paper in a little envelope. You then engage your 5-10 friends and give them a brief and ask them to write 6 sentences on what they think of you. You must emphasize that the more honest they are the more they will help you. Stress that you are not searching for compliments you are on a quest for understanding or simply say it is an assignment from a distance coach. Something that will make them feel comfortable because you want to get the most honest answer you can to help you move forward.

You then collate the answers if let's say you get 5 people, friends, family to respond to this exercise then you will of course have your survey results. I

> **Imagination is more important that knowledge.**
>
> *Albert Einstein*

NOTES:

'I am taking regular, visible, positive actions in my life.'

Sadly an oil spill hit the island and the whole population had to be moved to mainland Bali. All 176 inhabitants including Samuel and his family had to move and they sailed away from the island holding only their basic belongings not

must say when I have conducted this exercise with people I work with and coaching clients they are, in the eyes of 'other people', better, stronger; a little bit different from the way they perceive themselves. Hey, if anything emerges which is a shock, you are entitled to dig and delve and seek further understanding. However, it may simply be best to reflect upon the answers and accept that the world likes you. If there are any shockers it may be best to sit down with a coach or if you don't have one, your most trusted friend, and ask for help to understand. You are you. You then have a decision as to whether you wish to work to change the world's perception of you. That is your call. You are your own PR company after all!

How you like to learn

The next step is to understand how you like to learn. Many people have been in the corporate world and have been through batteries of tests to understand about their learning styles. The issue here is that despite the learning style identified by the corporations, the courses, workshops and seminars you attend for the rest of your life still don't necessarily sync with what learning style you need! By that I mean you don't turn up to a workshop and say "By the way I learn best this way so please conduct the workshop in a way to honour my learning style" do you!

It was Edward De Bono who categorised the learning styles into four ways we like to consider new knowledge.

| **Live to learn and you will learn to live.** |
| **Portuguese Proverb** |

NOTES:

'I am becoming a master of my own life, I am the designer.'

---

knowing when and if they would ever return to their home. This was a heart-wrenching experience for them all and yet the excitement of moving to the mainland and life in modern society tended to help the hurt in Samuel's mind

Why?
Does it work/happen/have to be so.

What is it?
What works/happens/that has to be so?

What if?
It doesn't work/doesn't happen/isn't the way.

How?
How does it work/happen/have to be so.

De Bono considered that we wear one of these 4 'hats' and I must confess that when I approach learning I comply with one of these hats or a mixture of these hats with one lead learning style and a secondary and tertiary style. You might wish to consider how you approach new learning.

The WHY person needs to understand the motivation and the benefits of this new knowledge. Ask yourself: What are the benefits of learning this? What will it help me to do/be/have?

The WHAT IF person wants to understand all the downsides to the knowledge, the risks and how things are covered if things go wrong or do not comply to the

rule of the model or the protocol. Ask yourself: What are the risks here? What if things go wrong?

> **The intelligent man is one who has successfully fulfilled many accomplishments, and is yet willing to learn more.**
>
> *Ed Parker*

NOTES:

'I am continually adding self-empowering beliefs to my life.'

---

as they sailed away in a UN Recovery ship.

Samuel was sent to one of the big Bali secondary schools, a good school with average results but renowned for being a little violent and aggressive. So after the initial

The HOW person wants to know the exact nature and detail of all the working parts in order to accept the

knowledge. Ask yourself: What are the details of how it works? What are the in and outs and full detail?

The WHAT IS IT person wants to fully understand the intricate details of everything in the tiniest detail down to the minutiae. Ask yourself: Exactly how does it work? What is the basis of it? What does it do and what are its benefits.

These hats are fine and to a certain extent they help one understand how we process information and indeed retain it. It helps us decide whether to embark on a project or not and it allows us to consider the risks in a balanced way. But there is a problem. Sometimes the old adage of 'he who shouts loudest wins' can be dangerous, especially in a group of individuals all considering one task. We all have a preferred hat we like to wear. If one of the hat wearers is disproportionately strong it can skew the decision-making process so much so that it actually prevents any action at all.

You could grade yourself. When making a decision on a scale of 1-10. 1 being the least important and 10 being the most important "where are you":

When learning I like to know the WHY

I need to know the benefits 1-2-3-4-5-6-7-8-9-10

The pessimist sees difficulty in every opportunity. The optimist sees opportunity in every difficulty.
Winston Churchill

NOTES:

'I am constantly moving things forward in my life.'

novelty of being the "new boy" he started to get into fights with the other boys of his age. This was certainly not the Samuel of the "old world". He tended to have no fear going into these fights no matter how much bigger his opponents

I need to understand all the risks
1-2-3-4-5-6-7-8-9-10

I need to know exactly what it is
1-2-3-4-5-6-7-8-9-10

I need to know how it works
1-2-3-4-5-6-7-8-9-10

Failure is only the opportunity to begin again more intelligently.

Henry Ford

Ok, so if you have answered as honestly as you can you now know what you are like in terms of the hat you like to wear. May I suggest that when you are making a decision from time to time, particularly a serious one, you may wish to grab other people into your team with other learning styles so that you can consider a problem or an issue with balance and depth of insight. Very much in line with De Bono's four hats.

What can go wrong with some people? Rather than having a balanced 'hat-wearing' they have a thing called 'distortion'. This is generally through no fault of their own. This is created by current conditioning, past conditioning and past consequences. This can create a great fear to act and a mental requirement to dig in on the area that they are most comfortable in. An example would be that fear may make the 'what is it' person so hell-bent on knowing all the detail that the length of time it takes to do all the research may mean an

NOTES:

'*I am on a constant quest to be the best I can possibly be.*'

were. He didn't understand the banter amongst the other boys and he certainly didn't understand the negative jibes being thrown at him. It simply was not part of the world he was used to. One day he became involved in

opportunity has been lost. I think the famous phrase is 'analysis is paralysis'. Another great description is that these people like to ensure 'all the lights are green' before proceeding. The same is true of the other hat wearers by the way too! An extreme position on any of them can create issues.

To break this habit, or indeed habits being entrenched, you may wish to consider working with a team of other hat wearers.

Step 1.

Understand how you learn and make decisions and what hat you prefer to wear.

Step 2.

Look to see how balanced this hat is compared with others.

Step 3.

Consider the basis of this hat position based on your life to date.

Step 4.

Seek out hat wearers who have a different way to look at the world. The skill is now combining your self-knowledge and decision-making style, with your personality style. So

> **The difference between perseverance and obstinacy is that the one often comes from a strong will, and the other from a strong won't.**
>
> *Henry Ward Beecher*

NOTES:

'I am accepting and applying new learning every day.'

a big fight and he was summoned to the Principal's office.

The Principal questioned him on why he was being so badly behaved and so he explained that we was always telling the other boys to take off their dark glasses

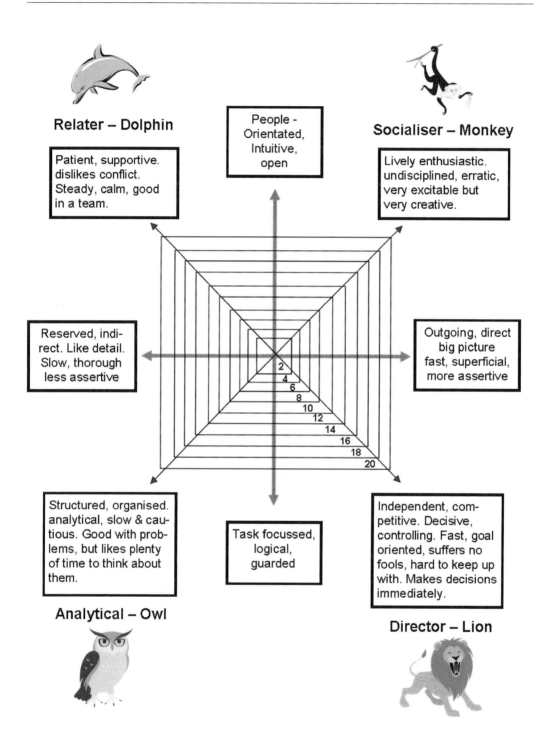

Relater – Dolphin

Patient, supportive. dislikes conflict. Steady, calm, good in a team.

People - Orientated, Intuitive, open

Socialiser – Monkey

Lively enthusiastic. undisciplined, erratic, very excitable but very creative.

Reserved, indirect. Like detail. Slow, thorough less assertive

Outgoing, direct big picture fast, superficial, more assertive

2
4
6
8
10
12
14
16
18
20

Structured, organised. analytical, slow & cautious. Good with problems, but likes plenty of time to think about them.

Task focussed, logical, guarded

Independent, competitive. Decisive, controlling. Fast, goal oriented, suffers no fools, hard to keep up with. Makes decisions immediately.

Analytical – Owl

Director – Lion

life is never simple and yet, to be fair, it is actually. By understanding yourself to the core you are being true to yourself! So look at your personality styles. One way to look at this is by using animals, I like this method (see previous page). It allows you to see your one or two preferred thinking

and acting styles in life. That is not to say you don't have skills in all these areas, but my research shows me that we definitely have two styles we prefer to use.

Your understanding of who you are and how you work will help guide you on your decision-making process. Being self-aware is so very important to allowing us confidence in our journey forward.

Am I making the right decision?

What if it's the wrong decision?

Let me help. Decision-making, learning styles and personality styles are very different. There has been a very holistic approach and indeed a whole educational marketing company launched which encapsulates a personality profiling method which defines who we are, what we should be doing and how we should be doing it in order to gain wealth, success and happiness. I applaud anyone or organisation which strives to help individuals reach an understanding of themselves. I have however, seen so many versions, (and all the companies insist that theirs is the right way), my advice is to learn and then

It's always too soon to quit. *David T Scoates*

NOTES:

'I am consolidating my knowledge and taking action on this knowledge every day.'

and see the real world. This confused the Principal and he retorted that none of the boys were even allowed to wear dark glasses and so he could not see the relevance of the defence Samuel had come up with! Samuel explained. "They

take stock and adopt the 'self understanding' methodology which helps you the most.

Intelligences

There are many coaches, authors, psychologists and motivational speakers who talk about 'Intelligences'. They categorise them into sectors to help us identify

where we are in our growth curve, in our personal development and in our journey. This is covered very well by one of my favourite authors, Malcolm Gladwell in *The Tipping Point*.

Grade yourself on a scale of 1 – 10 (1 being very low, 10 being very high) against these intelligences.

Practical Intelligence – how good are you at looking at and solving practical issues clearly, quickly and correctly?

1   2   3   4   5   6   7   8   9   10

Analytical Intelligence – how good are you at taking on analytical data, absorbing information and applying it for use?

1   2   3   4   5   6   7   8   9   10

> **You must always be resolutely determined that whatever you do shall always be the best of which you are capable.**
> **Charles E Popplestone**

NOTES:

> *'I am consistently gaining benefits from every element of learning I am involved in.'*

wear dark glasses in their minds. If they took off the glasses and could see the beauty of the world without all the (negative) clouds they would be much happier.

Samuel went on to explain "I come from a place where we seek to be positive,

Social Intelligence – how good are you at social interaction, meeting new people, existing acquaintances and communicating with ease?

1   2   3   4   5   6   7   8   9   10

Emotional Intelligence – How good are you at understanding and balancing your emotions to events that happen good and bad?

1   2   3   4   5   6   7   8   9   10

Strategic Intelligence – how good are you at mapping out options, ways forward, plans in advance for business, personal goals issues?

1   2   3   4   5   6   7   8   9   10

Spiritual Intelligence – how good are you at understanding your self, gaining spiritual equilibrium, balance, calm understanding of one's self.

1   2   3   4   5   6   7   8   9   10

This is not an exam it is, as mentioned before, the ability to understand who you are, and where you are in the world. I have met some people who are way off the scale in one form of intelligence but very low in others. How would I suggest you use this intelligence audit? Perhaps in the areas where, based on your

> **Everyone thinks of changing the world, but no one thinks of changing himself.**
>
> *Leo Tolstoy*

NOTES:

'I am crafting my own life my way.'

we seek to improve and we seek to find solutions. I just want these boys to take off their dark glasses inside their hearts and see the world from a positive place rather than thinking that we all start in a bad place". The Principal remained

subjective view, you scored low, set up a personal development goal to improve those scores. For example, let's imagine I have scored myself 4 out of 10 on the emotional intelligence scale. I would set out a goal for the following year to seek to improve this score with help, guidance, seminars, reading or mentors.

What we are considering becomes clearer as we set out on this journey of growth. We establish personal development goals to improve these intelligences by practice, by application or by the use of a coach or mentor to guide you through some regular exercises to help move you forward.

What was it someone once said, "work harder on yourself than you do on your work"? This is where the 90/10 rule also applies in my view. If you spend 10% of your life planning and also seeking to UNDERSTAND yourself the other 90% will be more effective than you can possibly believe. There are certainly so many dimensions in personal growth to consider, spiritual growth, emotional growth, discovery and maturity. My advice is to understand all these areas of growth and from time to time simply embrace the growth of the intelligences within you and your power of self-awareness, and be aware in which area or areas your growth is occurring. Sadly it's not like school. It's not a maths lesson then a geography lesson. All the interpersonal growth subjects intertwine. But I am not worried for you. Humans are very intelligent animals and we can handle it!

> **Destiny is not a matter of chance; it is a matter of choice. It is not a thing to be waited for; it is a thing to be achieved.**
> *William Jennings Bryan*

NOTES:

'I am in control of what I think, feel, say and do.'

silent for some time knowing that he had heard a very valid point and over the next few weeks set about implementing a culture of honest feedback, positive and constructive advice and encouragement to all pupils and funnily enough

I suspect that a Neuro Linguistic Programming (NLP) Master Practitioner would turn in his grave if I simply said "sure NLP has its part in all this". But the understanding of how we interpret and file information from the input of the world is also key. Apparently we have three preferred styles or preferred interpretation methods for filtering information into our world:

We feel - Kinaesthetic

We see – Visual

We hear – Auditory

There is a fourth which is Olfactory the sense of smell and this also features in the way we digest the world and record our memories for reference in the future.

You will know instinctively which one you prefer to use in your world. Simply reflect upon your last holiday. You will remember it either by the way you felt, or the sounds of the best memories of that time, or you will recall the sights of the holiday. That's your clue.

Ok so let's try to hang all this together. In the form of matrices (see over):

Remember what Socrates said - the key to life is to 'know thyself'. I personally believe that your journey can progress so much better if you take the steps to understand who you are and where you sit in the world!

> **There are no secrets to success. It is the result of preparation, hard work, and learning from failure.**
>
> *Colin L Powell*

NOTES:

'I am continually looking to be self-aware, self-controlling, self managing.'

Samuel never got into another fight again and the reputation of the school escalated beyond compare.

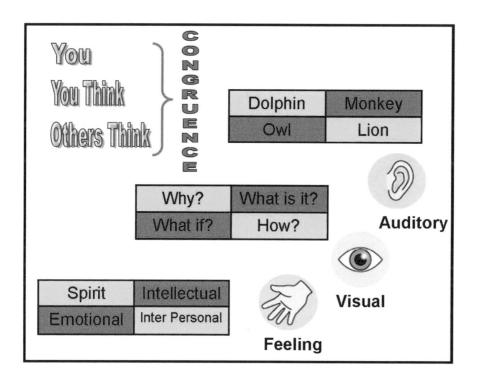

Chapter 1 Summary

So you can take action with this knowledge by conducting a self-awareness exercise on yourself and then asking some good friends to be honest and to help you. You can identify how you like to learn and take information on board. You can identify which two personality styles you prefer to favour, and apply these to everyday life all the time. You can use your knowledge of how to interpret the world in terms of your senses – feeling, seeing, hearing. You can also see where you sit in your various 'intelligences'. How do you apply this understanding of yourself? Someone once said "Quite simply walk with more understanding and wisdom through your garden." Be yourself, tap into your strengths and don't beat yourself up if there are things you simply can't do or don't do.

Now let's dive into how all these component parts came to make YOU in the first place – the 3 'C's'.

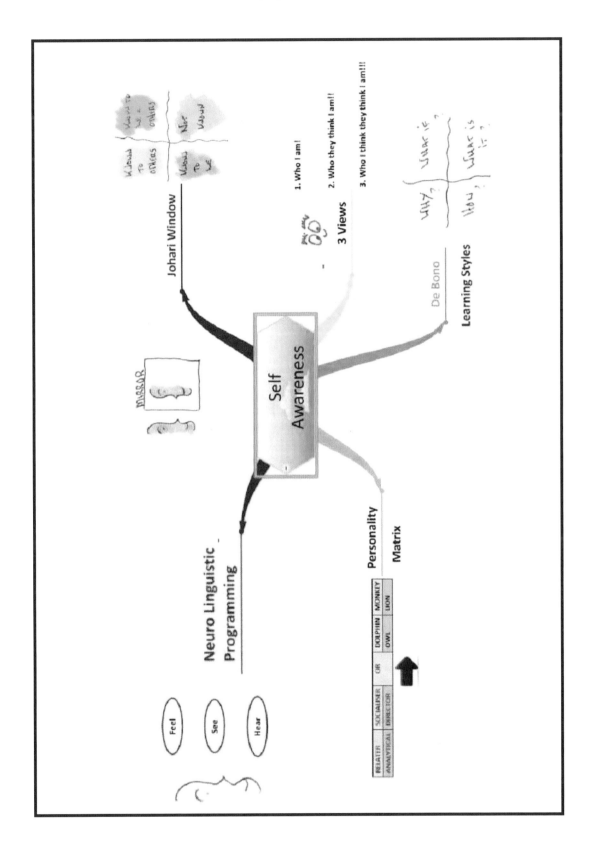

Chapter 2

The Three 'C's'

A glimpse at:-

- Fears
- Conditioning
- Confidence
- Consequences
- Brain input

> Remember, no more effort is required to aim high in life, to demand abundance and prosperity, than is required to accept misery and poverty.
> **Napoleon Hill**

NOTES:

As I walked through the park the other day with my dog Ollie who was busy investigating every tree, leaf and blade of grass, I put away my affirmation cards and I pondered upon one particular question:

"What is the difference between people making dramatic progress in life and those who never change?"

Incidentally, the use of affirmation cards is one of the methods I have used for many years and they are one of the many 'handrails of success' that I have embedded into my life and I will share how invaluable these are with you later in the book.

'I am embracing every new challenge which I may come across.'

Pebbles in a Jar

A lecturer was addressing a group of students in Cardiff University. The students were used to the lecturer using props and metaphors to illustrate a point in their psychology class so they always went along with his games.

Fear has many shapes, forms and colours and is borne out of an adopted collection of experiences and imposed values that we have collected together and stored neatly in the filing cabinets of our brain.

Now back to the question I had posed myself, or indeed pose to you, as I bet you are thinking about it now too.

One of the conclusions I came to is that there are many barriers to success or progress and the greatest one that I have seen is 'Fear'. Those who are moving forward have learned how to manage or overcome their fears but I need to state two things here:

1. Its **OK** to have fears!
2. There **ARE** ways to either overcome or bypass these fears!

Let's have a look at these fears; see where they come from and decide how to deal with them.

Have you ever forgotten to let the hand brake off when heading out on a drive? I have and it made me feel embarrassed even though I was alone in the car. My progress was hampered but I saw the red light on the dashboard, released the handbrake and away I went as if I had pressed 'turbo- drive'.

Well, Fear is the handbrake of your brain; if you don't let it go it will hamper your progress forward.

> **To accomplish great things, we must not only act, but also dream; not only plan, but also believe.**
>
> *Anatole France*

NOTES:

'I am developing positive mental muscles every single day of my life.'

He pulled out a glass jar about a foot and a half high which was see-though and made of thickened glass. He proceeded to fill the jar with large stones about 3-4 inches wide.

He kept going until the stones were up to the top of the jar…

Fear is an emotion that we put in place to protect us against danger. Once we understand and accept this we can make a rational decision as to whether it is a logical or illogical emotion and deal with it accordingly.

The best way to see our way through the fear block is to use tools to check whether the fear stands the 'logic' test.

Firstly we need to establish the type of fear and where it comes from;

There are 3 main categories:

Conditioning –
  ➤ Is it from your upbringing? Has it been instilled into you from your first breath right up to the point you are now?

  ➤ Is it from your environment? Is it from the culture in which you live which creates the boundaries of behaviour you work within?

  ➤ Is it from a previous bad experience? Does this underpin the reason why you shouldn't do something?

  ➤ Is it from others? Does a situation or an individual continually condition you to think or act in a way that doesn't really match the real you?

> **The only thing that will grow is the thing we give energy to.**
>
> *Ralph Waldo Emerson*

NOTES:

'I am achieving superb things by taking small steps forward every single day.'

"Is it full?" He said addressing his eager-eyed students
"No" they said.

So he pulled out a bag of pebbles and continued to fill the jar. Slowly but surely the pebbles filled in the gaps between the big stones until he could not fit any

Confidence –

➢ Could fear arise from the fact that a skill or process you need to perform a task is, in your view, lacking?

➢ Is it because you feel convinced that you will not do as well at a particular task as you would like to do?

➢ Do you feel that you don't have enough knowledge to complete your task?

➢ Could it simply be that the last time you tried a particular task you failed?

Consequences –

➢ Do you fear being teased or worse, humiliated, as a result of an action or performance not going well?

➢ Might it be based on negative affirmations? Have you been told so often that if you do something it will be bad?

➢ We all need re-assurance, so if you are not getting any this could be why you don't want to do anything.

➢ We are often our own worst critic so maybe you have been pilloried   so much that you are no longer prepared to try?

Let's have a look at each of these areas in more detail. I'm going to give you a story for each from which we can draw our own conclusions and then create a cons-

> **Hate and fear can poison the body as surely as any toxic chemicals.**
>
> *Joseph Krimsky M.D.*

NOTES:

'I am seeking solutions to any large or difficult hurdles I come across.'

---

more stones in.

"Is it full"? He said smiling knowingly. "No" they said

So he pulled out a bag of sand and proceeded to pour in the sand which filled

tructive survival action plan to deal with the fear that has been created.

Conditioning - Up-Bringing

a) Negative story:
My father was a major in the army in Singapore just before they gained independence so 2-3 years before the British Empire broke its links with Singapore. I was aged 9-10 and my passion was swimming. I had the opportunity to swim every day for hours and hours so I was pretty good. I really loved competing which I did at every given opportunity and I clocked up a few medals and awards along the way. The funny thing is I don't remember my father ever coming to watch me in any of my events!

How did this negatively condition me?
I built up a continual 'need' to 'make him proud' of me; maybe then he would take an interest. Strange in a way I suppose but the rationale and the purpose were drawn from the negative need to be approved of and the continual need for reassurance created a 'negative conditioning' in as much as I was not content with competing for my own pleasure; I was doing it to get 'noticed'.

Lesson;
Whatever it is, do it for your own sake, and for the right reasons.

Action:
When you decide to do something, establish the correct motivation.

> **Happiness lies in the joy of achievement and the thrill of creative effort.**
> *Franklin Roosevelt*

NOTES:

'I am feeling joyful and brimming with pride as I take charge of my life.'

---

in the spaces in between the big stones and the pebbles and he kept going until the sand spilled over the top of the jar.

"Is it full?" he said, by now giggling to himself
"No" they all said in unison.

b) Positive story:

It is often said that our deepest values are embedded in us by the time we reach 7 or 8 years of age; politeness and respect for example; if I did not use my pleases and thank you's as a child I would be regularly and continually reminded of the phrase 'Manners Maketh The Man' by both mum and dad.

I am eternally grateful for this conditioning as I never ever forget now and when I do thank someone I really try to wrap the thanks in 'genuine tone'. The expression of genuine thanks well meant really does do wonders in the world. I thank my parents for this gift.

Live to learn and you will learn to live.

Portuguese Proverb

NOTES:

'*I am displaying self-courage every day.*'

"Ok" he said what we shall do now?

"Let's get some water" they all said as some of them had seen a demonstration of this type before and they thought they knew what he was going to say about this exercise.

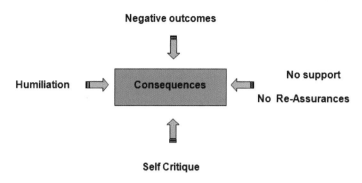

Conditioning – A closer look:

My position is that conditioning, be it positive or negative, is a key factor in whether or not we bump into and feel fear. If we look closely at conditioning it can be categorised as positive, negative or indeed neutral. Nevertheless it is a process which causes input into the brain which predefines and therefore frames our response to an identical circumstance in the future. Have you noticed that people react so differently to the same situation?

☹ - Negative ⇨ 👤 ⇦ Positive + ☺

Conditioning can come from a variety of directions and remains a continuous process throughout our whole lives. This conditioning becomes embedded in our sub-conscious and it is the reference library we use to make decisions.

NOTES:

'I am self-aware and I am always loving myself.'

So obedient to the cause the professor reached under the podium from where he was addressing the students and pulled out a jar of water. He filled the jar with water until the water dribbled over the top.

As a child I once played around with a box of matches, and of course as children do, I made a mistake – a very painful one! I held a burning match which I found pretty, fascinating and exciting; I held on for too long and of course I burned my finger. It was a sharp harsh pain which I have never forgotten. The lesson I learned? Yup! If you play with fire you will get burned, and it will hurt.

There are other lessons too; It's ok to play with matches; it's ok to enjoy looking at the fire, watching it flicker and spit is great fun but, care is needed - there is a finite time to enjoy the experience before it will do you harm.

The 'burning match' experience for me was one of the millions of 'conditioning processes' that I have experienced in my life which have helped to protect me, guide me and take me through experience with as little harm as possible.

If we can learn these lessons and learn to trust what they are teaching us we can use them in the future as reference points that will become part of our 'manual of life'. The input we get from our conditioning actually controls the way we interpret the world and actions and reactions every second of the day.

> **The pessimist sees difficulty in every opportunity. The optimist sees opportunity in every difficulty.**
>
> *Winston Churchill*

NOTES:

'I am embracing every day with joy and happiness.'

"Is it full now?" He asked in a slightly teasing manner.

The students shuffled uneasily because they were also aware the professor could be a little bit of a tease. So some said no, some said yes, and some did not answer.

Let's take a closer look at Confidence:

Confidence, or rather lack of it is a key element of fear that I see in the clients I coach and teach. It's a tricky one as it manifests itself in many different forms.

"If only I had the confidence to ...". Well, if only I'd had a pound for every time I've heard those words!

Confidence is based on the reference library in our brain with which we predict either logically or illogically the outcome of any given situation. If it is a negative prediction our confidence is automatically lowered even though we cannot see into the future and don't know what will actually happen.

There are many ways of increasing confidence which we will address at a later stage, but we must realise that this lack of confidence nurtures fear, for an overview of this let's look at one instance of the confidence progression.

I am currently embarking on a new challenge which involves learning a new skill – that of public speaking. Now although I mastered the art of speaking some time ago; I have established and prepared the material I am delivering and I practice for hours and hours, I'm still scared when I perform.

The first time I did OK and graded myself 3/10 and in essence I did not enjoy it. This left me at a crossroads; do I continue trying to improve in the

> **Our greatest weakness lies in giving up. The most certain way to succeed is to always try first one more time.**
> *Thomas Edison*

NOTES:

'I am proud of my ability to learn and grow all the time.'

The professor smiled and then pulled out a salt cellar and began very slowly to pour the salt on top the top of the water which had soaked through the big rocks, the pebbles and the sand. Sure enough the salt was absorbed by the water until the surplus gathered on the top.

hope that I will get better and therefore enjoy it more, or, do I give up?

This is a complicated matter to consider. We already have:

➢ Knowledge Learned
➢ Skills Learned / Shown
➢ Skills Practised

Regardless of the methods, training essentially follows the classic learning path of:

Told – Shown – Tried

Learning matrix diagram

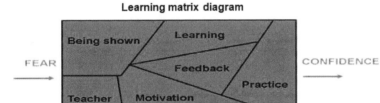

I decided to continue training and get better at public speaking. The confidence curve increased every time I presented. I always asked for feedback and guidance from peers, friends and colleagues (all feedback is positive).

I concentrated to begin with on one particular presentation. I delivered this over and over again until I

> He who stops being better stops being good.
>
> *Oliver Cromwell*

NOTES:

'I am matching everything I do to my prime purpose in life.'

"Is it full now?"
"Yes" they all said not really seeing his point!

became so comfortable with the material and the delivery style that I actually relaxed into the skill. I realised that I was now enjoying what I was doing.

I now enjoy all my public speaking engagements and feel a huge sense of pride as I leave the platform. What is the key? The knowledge? Yes. The teacher? Yes. The practice? Yes. The support? Yes. The motivation? Yes. The persistence? Yes. It's all of these which make up the jigsaw puzzle of instilling confidence during a passage through the fear barrier!

Let's take a closer look at Consequences:

It's not that I'm saying we shouldn't consider the consequences of what we do; nor am I suggesting for one second that that we should not listen to the voices of wisdom coming into our minds based on our experiences. Our past experiences and the wisdom gained from them rightly or wrongly decide how we correctly anticipate what will happen if we take a particular path in life, take an action or make a decision.

What I am saying is that any fear factor must be tempered with a logical process based on one definite - we cannot see what WILL happen. We can use all the examples in the reference library and give exactly identical situations with exactly the same behaviour and potentially expect the same results. But, consider this: we all change all the time as do others and as does the environment and therefore it will NEVER be the same. Life moves on.

> **Destiny is not a matter of chance; it is a matter of choice. It is not a thing to be waited for; it is a thing to be achieved.**
> *William Jennings Bryan*

NOTES:

'I am matching everything I do to my prime purpose in life.'

"What am I trying to demonstrate"? he asked the collective body and one or two keen students put their hands up straight away and gave comments about time-planning; building you day around the main things and then letting the minor

The danger is that if we anticipate the consequences with the wrong brief and use a reference library which has for years been filled with some 'corrupted files' (I'm using my extensive IT knowledge here), then the anticipation becomes flawed. The fear is therefore 'potentially false'.

I set up my own business in 2003 and walked out of the office where I had been effectively employed for 2½ years, much like the business I had previously worked in for 14 years. I had shown commitment, loyalty and respect throughout those years and the guiding advice I received was 'It's tough out there; with all the support you get here you would be mad to try and go it alone.'

This constant message of reassurance and negative affirmation of the consequences of setting up my own business, had put an anchor on my motives and built a 'wall of intellectual fear' around me.

So why did I still decide to jump in the end? I took a long hard look at the jigsaw puzzle and decided that I was ready. It took me 16½ years to get to that point. I have no regrets but I would be intrigued to see if without the constant negative affirmations I would have been ready to make the jump sooner, say after 2 years, 5 years, but certainly I feel it would not have taken me over 16 years.

> **The difference between a successful person and others is not a lack of strength, lot a lack of knowledge, but rather a lack of will.**
> *Vince Lombardi*

NOTES:

'I am able to command and control the way I handle situations.'

things in-fill the day and if you don't place the big rocks in the jar first your planning will not work etc.

The professor agreed that that was the original theme of the demonstration.

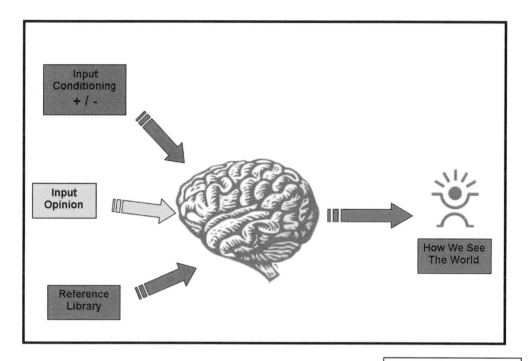

Going back to the fear that we are potentially looking to overcome, one of the key elements is to metaphorically 'walk around' the fear and test it's authenticity by asking some questions:

- What is this fear?
- Is it a real fear?
- Where does this fear come from?
- Can we overcome this fear?
- Do we want to overcome this fear?

Its OK to have fears, we all do! The key is to understand them and keep them in perspective.

NOTES:

'I am regularly energised by my belief in my ability to succeed.'

But he went on to explain that that particular day he wanted to talk about attitude. So he pulled out some light blue ink and poured it into the jar and the light blue coloured all the contents of the jar with a superb bright blue .

Lets go back and look at our fears again and this time lets consider the 'biggies'. The ones that are the most common are:

- Fear of failure
- Fear of success
- Fear of ill health
- Fear of dying
- Fear of loss

> You gain strength, courage and confidence by every experience by which you really stop to look fear in the face. You are able to say to yourself "I lived through this horror, I can take the next thing that comes along."
> *Eleanor Roosevelt*

The one that always surprises people is the 'Fear of success' because it is not such an obvious one, nevertheless it is a highly dominant one and a lot of individuals might say that they lack success in one arena or another but they are actually resistant to the idea of change when they get there!

How do we find out our fears, learn to accept them, come to terms with them, and even overcome them? Well, some will attend training courses and complete exercises regularly, learning tactics to help them face fears as they appear, while others will think they can do it without help. Here is a little exercise that I've put together for you have a go at. It doesn't take long and you'll be amazed at the results if you answer the questions honestly:

Grade yourself on the fear factor, (1 is no fear at all – 10 is absolutely terrified). It is rare and perhaps dangerous to have no fear at all so don't be too bullish and remember of course if you want to 'hide from yourself' you can always pretend and make up the answers but I would then have to ask you "What are you afraid of?"

NOTES:

'I am taking command of every minute of every day.'

The professor explained that this was a perfectly crafted day/week/month/year. Planned, prioritized and organized to maximise success with a positive (light blue slant) attitude weaved within the master plan.

Fear Factor	1	2	3	4	5	6	7	8	9	10
1. You are asked to do a presentation to a groupnof 20 people on a subject you know well and you have 2 weeks to prepare.										
2. You are asked to step in and give a presentation with 5 minutes notice.										
3. Dying.										
4. Becoming seriously ill.										
5. Break up in your closest personal relationship.										
6. Loss of a partner.										
7. Loss of a job.										
8. Loss of your business.										
9. Great financial loss.										
10. Robbery or personal assault.										
11. Failing to progress										
12. Success.										
13. Meeting new people socially.										
14. Making mistakes that will cost money.										
15. Making mistakes that will hurt other people.										

Okay, now add up your scores. Whether you scored 15 or 150 it doesn't really matter. It only matters that you are aware of the fears. List the top 5 fears now in terms of highest scoring:

1.
2.
3.
4.
5.

Now add a few of your own fears that weren't on my list:

1.
2.
3.
4.
5.

By the way it's OK to have fears as long as you understand what they are and why you have them. You can live with them or deal with them and hopefully overcome them, but it's your choice. You could actually put together a plan based on your list of fears and set about overcoming these. What is it they say - "Fear is temporary but regret is forever". You can leave it or deal with it. You could take one fear a year, (or month), to deal with.

You can feed or starve fear. By feeding fear you allow your thoughts to engulf you and keep you back. The key action here is to avoid placing yourself in a fear situation until you are ready. But when you are ready

> **Ships in harbour are safe, but that's not what ships are built for.**
>
> *John Shedd*

NOTES:

'I am taking time to take stock and enjoy the moment as I walk my journey.'

He then addressed the students again and explained that the black ink he held in his hand was indicative of a "negative moment" he placed the bottle of ink over the jar and dropped in 3 drops of black ink only.

take the next step.

I find that what has helped me through 100% of my fears is simply to hold someone's hand literally or metaphorically speaking. It's scary on your own but not when holding someone's hand who has overcome the same fear.

> **Pessimism is a poison and optimism is a magnet, and if you can deal with that you manage.**
>
> *Anna Massey*

'I am taking command of every minute of every day.'

The jar turned black as did all its contents.

"What do we think of this people?" he asked.

Chapter 2 Summary

So we have looked at the factors which bring us to where we are today and this is clearly not a simple matter. But by understanding how and why we feel as we do, and react as we do, we can get to grips with life a lot better. Like an actor going on stage for the first performance, the actor has learned their lines 100%. Having learned our lines we now have to react to the audience, (real life). How do we apply this knowledge? Self-understanding is vital so work really hard on this area. Now let's have a look at some of our beliefs and how they shape our lives.

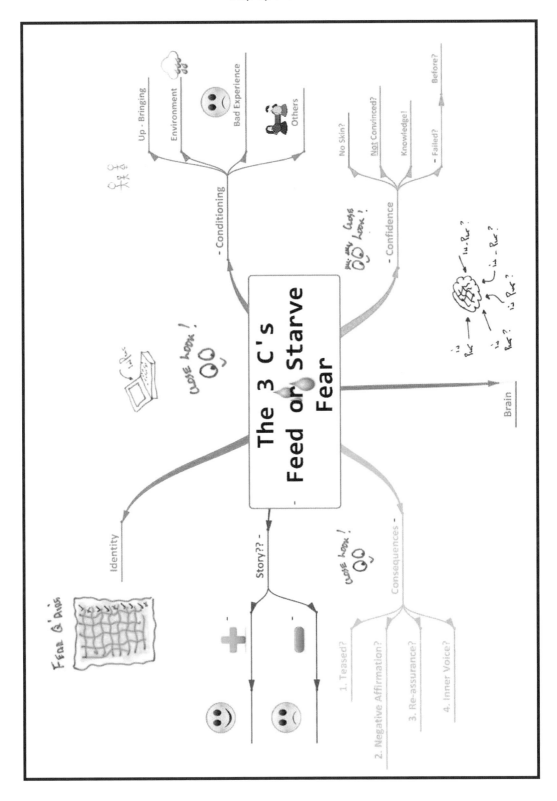

The 3 C's
Feed or Starve Fear

Chapter 3

Positive and Negative Beliefs

A glimpse at:-

- Self-limiting beliefs
- Self-limiting phrases
- Self-limiting actions
- Self-limiting patterns

NOTES:

There are a mixture of limiting factors that can put the brakes on everything we do in life. We can look at these manifested in several ways:

- Self Limiting Beliefs (SLB's)
- Self Limiting Phrases (SLP's)
- Self Limiting Actions (SLA's)

Which form Self Limiting *Patterns*.

Provided we look at and fully understand how these features affect our life then we can actually change those things! Some of these SLB's, SLP's and SLA's are well entrenched and have been part of us for years and can be so embedded in our lives they can linger around for a long time. But it is the awareness and understanding of these that helps guide us away from

'I am not super-human but I am a pretty super human!'

Dances with Wolves

A white-haired Cherokee is teaching his grandchildren about life.

these features. Someone once said "practice makes perfect" but also "practice can make *permanent*".

In the background to living this life each day, the first awareness that is required is that we have a daily flow of negative or limiting thoughts. A variety of studies and authors have issued a variety of numerical figures concerned with the amount of automatic negative thoughts that flow into our minds during, (supposedly), our waking hours. I have seen a figure of 40,000–60,000 of these thoughts a day. Where do they come from? Well let's track one of these and what might happen!

- We have a thought hit our mind "I am not going to do very well here."
- This is underpinned by one of our self-limiting beliefs "I don't normally do very well in these situations."
- This is possibly negatively affirmed by a little self-limiting phrase issued out loud "I don't usually do well at this."
- The body and mind now take over and turn this into a behavioural feature and we approach the whole situation physically and behaviourally in a pre-determined way. The result is it <u>doesn't</u> go well.

This is a clear *Self Limiting Pattern*.

We can look at the model which may paint the picture of what happens.

> **Everything is possible for those who believe.**
>
> *Mark 9:23*

NOTES:

'I am consciously planning my life to ensure it has direction and purpose.'

He tells them, "A fight is going on inside me; a terrible fight,

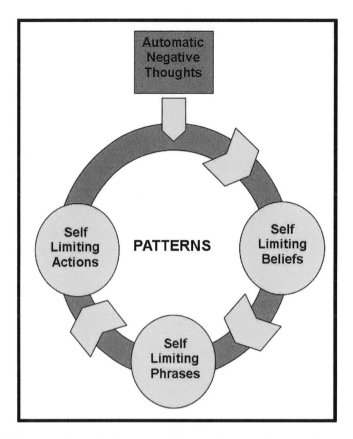

Destiny is no matter of chance. It is a matter of choice.

William Jennings Bryan

NOTES:

We need to look into this and consider quite simply whether we accept this as the way it is, or consider whether we would like to change direction; change the 'way it is'. In a similar way to approaching all things we can take action, the quandary could be where and how can we solve this problem. Where do we jump in and which area can we attack first?

We can actually attack these patterns at any point in this cycle.

'I am working all the time to be self-aware and aware of myself.'

and it is a fight between two wolves.

One of the key things is to recognise these A.N.T.s (Automatic Negative Thoughts) as soon as they arise, or reduce their arrival!

One way we could deal with these A.N.T.s is the way we set-up every day, by our daily routine and by giving ourselves the best chance of having the best day we can have.

The first hour of every day is key to establishing your mood, your mindset and your positivity for the rest of the day. I find that what works for me and many of my coaching clients is to have a series of rituals to start the day. For those avid rugby supporters, you'll be very familiar with the way the English rugby player Jonny Wilkinson prepares for every kick in every match in exactly the same way. We must do the same for our best day.

Here is a prompt that I use to encourage my clients to have a good think about their daily set up:-

(see next page)

Fill yourself with warrior spirit and send that warrior into action.

Jonny Wilkinson

NOTES:

'I am consciously ignoring all the disempowering thoughts I have.'

"One wolf represents fear, greed, hatred, anger, envy, false pride,

Daily Set Up

What do you currently do between getting up and getting to work?
What is it like?
How do you feel?
List the steps you take below:

1. **I wake up then I** _____

2. **Then I** _____

3. **Then I** _____

4. **Then I** _____

5. **Then I** _____

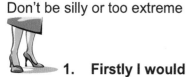 **I would say that I generally have a ___ /10 day**

NOW think about what tiny **steps you could take <u>EVERY</u> day (or nearly every day) that would give you the BEST possible chance of having a 10/10 day?**
Don't be silly or too extreme

1. **Firstly I would** _____

2. **Then I would** _____

3. **Then I would** _____

4. **Then I would** _____

5. **Then I would** _____

Then I would have a 10/10 day!!!

For example:

Daily Set Up

What do you currently do between getting up and getting to work?
What's it like?
How do you feel?
List the steps you take below:

1. I wake up then I press snooze on the alarm, twice.

2. Then I stay in my pyjamas and watch the breakfast TV.

3. Then I drink two cups of strong coffee and skip breakfast.

4. Then I miss my bus.

5. Then I arrive late for work, grumpy and apologetic.

 I would say that I generally have a 4 /10 day

NOW think about what tiny steps you could take EVERY day (or nearly every day) that would give you the BEST possible chance of having a 10/10 day?
Don't be silly or too extreme

1. Firstly I would get up as soon as the alarm goes off.

2. Then I would get washed and dressed.

3. Then I would have breakfast

4. Then I would listen to a motivational CD on the bus.

5. Then I would start the day with a clear and focussed 'to do' list.

Then I would have a 10/10 day!!!

One way to look at this is to imagine that you have placed a 'Star Trek' force field around you to ward off enemies!

If we can assume that we can attack these patterns at a variety of points, let's look at the SELF LIMITING BELIEFS. There are many writers, coaches and authors who have addressed this subject. One theory is that these SLB's emanate from a series of sources:-

- Social environment
- Authority figures
- Repetitious information
- Experiences
- Self image

No-one has the right to ruin my day, except me!

Nancy Regan

NOTES:

Social Environment

- Are there any experiences you have had in your life to date which have discouraged you and made you feel limited/negative?

  List them _____

  _____

- Are there a couple of instances in your life where you were made to feel silly? Uncared for? Un-intelligent?

  List them _____

  _____

'I am congratulating myself as I succeed in changing the shape of my life.'

self-pity, resentment, guilt, inferiority, arrogance, deceitfulness, superiority, and selfishness.

- Look at some of the environments you lived in where you were made to feel discouraged, worthless?

  Home (parents, now)/nursery, primary, secondary school, college, university, job 1, job 2, job 3, 4 ,5 etc.

  List them _____

  _____

> Men are anxious to improve their circumstances, but are unwilling to improve themselves; they therefore remain bound.
>
> *James Allen*

Authority Figures

Have a look at your world and who has influenced you in the past and who influences you at present? This is a tough call because you are being asked to look into to the very centre of your heart and some of your honesty may be painful to recognise!

Have these people or environments (in general) encouraged you or discouraged you in life?

Mother	Yes/No
Father	Yes/No
Brothers	Yes/No
Sisters	Yes/No
Relatives	Yes/No
School friends	Yes/No
College	Yes/No
University	Yes/No
Job 1	Yes/No
Job 2	Yes/No

NOTES:

'I am deliberately designing my life around my needs and wishes.'

"The other wolf stands for peace, love, kindness, joy, truth, compassion,

Job 3   Yes/No
Job 4   Yes/No
Job 5   Yes/No
Relationship partner   Yes/No

Self Image

How we see ourselves and how we therefore use the view of ourselves is key! Having a positive 'self image' without any blemishes in the 'perfect person' is easier said than done. There is a great movement at present in the world to encourage individuals to 'be themselves'. Don't understand this to be a form of arrogance or conceit, it is a determining factor in success and happiness. Earlier in the book we looked at the Johari window and saw that there are 3 you's!

- The way you see yourself.
- The way you think others see you.
- The way others actually see you.

The way to trial this is to be brave enough to actually go through this exercise and ask 5-10 people who you trust for your 5 best attributes, it will be interesting to see the results. By the way you can't argue what they think. The results will either confirm for you your vision of yourself or may even shock you into realising you are so much better than you thought!

Another thing you can do is kick the legs out from some of these self-limiting self-image beliefs. Answer some questions –

> **Excellence is the gradual result of always striving to do better.**
>
> *Pat Riley*

NOTES:

'I am trampling down any fears I had about my inability to change.'

humility, transparency, authenticity, friendship, respect, integrity, benevolence,

Do you ever have any of these feelings?

- Do you ever feel un-loved?
- Do you ever feel discouraged?
- Do you ever feel a failure?
- Do you ever feel you want to give up?
- Do you ever feel anxiety?
- Do you ever feel depressed?
- Do you ever feel stressed?

The paradox is this – to have more on the outside we must spend time on the inside.

Peter Field

If you do then the way to kick the legs out is a typical CBT (Cognitive Behavioural Therapy) technique, which is to look at these feelings in depth, by imagining that these feelings are built or supported by some table legs:

NOTES:

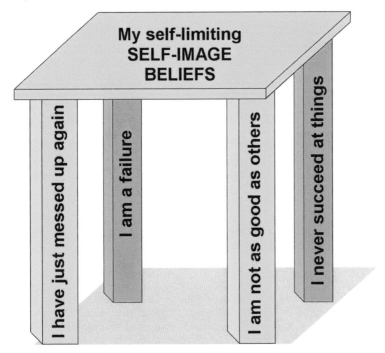

'I am allowing my needs and desires to take a place in my life planning.'

generosity, faith, sharing, serenity and empathy.

This table kicking can be great fun, let's kick this one away. Self-conversation goes a bit like this: imagine you are your own coach and you refuse to accept negativity and you challenge your table legs. If my inner voice was saying "I am a failure" then my inner coach would say as follows:

So let's just make a list of 10 things you have done in your whole life that you are proud of:

1.
2.
3.
4.
5.
6.
7.
8.
9.
10.

Ok, now take a moment and write 250 – 500 words on the proudest day of your life. Read often and even keep this 'prize page' in your wallet/handbag and bring it out as your positive grounding reminder to challenge your own self sometimes as a counter-argument to any table legs!

Now reflect back on the table legs.

Do these make sense? Do they have any validity? OK, so the answer is that you can chop up this particular table into firewood!

> **The life which is unexamined is not worth living.**
>
> *Plato*

NOTES:

'I am focused on making things happen that blend into my wishes.'

"The same fight is going on inside you and in every other person too."

Look, I know it's not easy. We have to work on ourselves all the time, but as we do, it does get easier, I promise you!

Repetitious Information

If you are told you are brilliant enough times you will begin to believe it and of course the truth is that if the opposite is said repeatedly enough, that becomes true as well. To a certain extent this breaks into the area of self-limiting patterns which I will cover shortly. However, the thing to do is to identify where this information comes from – people, friends, family, work colleagues, the TV, radio, web, news. I am fully aware that we are bombarded hourly by negatives and the destructive views of other people. This I can assure you, has a damaging effect on us and our opinions if we are not careful.

If we wake up one morning with a statement "This is a beautiful world, I am happy to be alive and today is going to be superb!", watch how quickly this view is challenged when you turn on the news on TV or radio or read the newspaper. How long? 10 minutes? 30 minutes? What I recommend is that you deliberately seek to avoid this negative input in a major way. You can design your own steps. These are mine:-

1. I am a very selective TV watcher.
2. I don't read newspapers.
3. I avoid negative people.
4. I detach from a crowd if there is a negative flow occurring.

> **By your thoughts you are daily, even hourly, building your life; you are carving your destiny.**
>
> **Ruth Barrick Golden**

NOTES:

'I am focused on achieving little changes to my life with simple steps.'

The children thought about this for a while.

So there you go! What four things will you do to protect yourself from all those flows of repetitious negative information:-

1.
2.
3.
4.

How will you ensure that you stick to this?

Experiences

Look, we all have bad things happen to us. But the key is how we deal with the bad things, how we recover, and how we then move on. So many writers, coaches and trainers have considered this aspect of ourselves. I certainly like the analogy of someone carrying a great big rucksack full of stories behind them as they try to move forward. Each and every story represents a negative experience someone has had. So why carry them all around with you?

My advice is to leave the rucksack behind! You can't go back! The bad thing happened, take a decision on how you will consider this, then move on!

So the message is very clear – garbage happens, then it's happened, take from it what you can to learn and move forward. Discard the rest.

> **Good thoughts and actions can produce bad results; bad thoughts and actions can never produce good results.**
> *James Allen*

NOTES:

'I am self-aware and understand that things will never be 100% perfect.'

Then one little girl asked her grandfather, "Which wolf will win?"

BAD THING HAPPENS

- Think about it ...

DECIDE WHAT YOU HAVE LEARNT

- Decide if in future your actions or thought process will change

ONWARDS AND UPWARDS!

- Put the negative thought behind you
- Look the world in the eye!
- Smile!
- Move on! Onwards and upwards!

> **The quality of your thoughts determines the quality of your life.**
>
> *Vera Peiffer*

NOTES:

Self-Limiting Phrases

Now there are strange little things which become so embedded into our way of life we hardly ever notice. I am sure there are more but have a look at the list on page 84.

Can you see how damaging these can be? What you might wish to consider is some active listening amongst your friends and family and identify who comes out with the most. Even better, listen to yourself! I am lucky enough to work with a group of people who have agreed to point out when an SLP is used and challenge them.

There are counters to these – let me give you an example:

> *'I am resolute in my determination to succeed in everything I do.'*

The old Cherokee held a long silence,

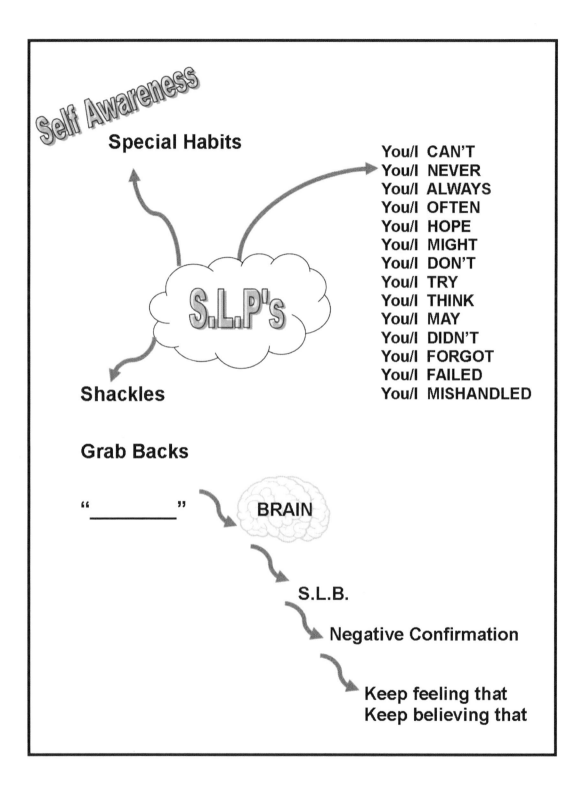

I can't	-	I can
I never	-	I always
I won't	-	I will
I'll try	-	I will
I think	-	I have decided
I may	-	I will

Do you see how effective taking an assertive tone in your vocabulary can change the mood. If you reflect back to even your last conversation with someone, you might identify with some amusement how accurate this is.

NOTES:

Self Limiting Actions

Self Limiting Actions (SLA's) form the last link between the other self limiting factors. An SLA is the purely physical behaviour which is translated from the mental messages and verbal messages we have created. It is therefore a case of what we actually do with this information.

- The board meeting – "who wants to take a lead on this?"
  The SLA is the refusal to volunteer to take the lead due to the SLB "I don't do too well at taking the lead" verbalised outwardly with the same SLP.
- The social invitation – "do you want to come to a networking meeting?"
  The SLA is the non-attendance, the SLB is the "I don't feel good at networking meetings" again underpinned by the outward verbalisation.

'I am creating a clear path towards achieving my goals.'

and then simply said, "Whichever one you feed"!

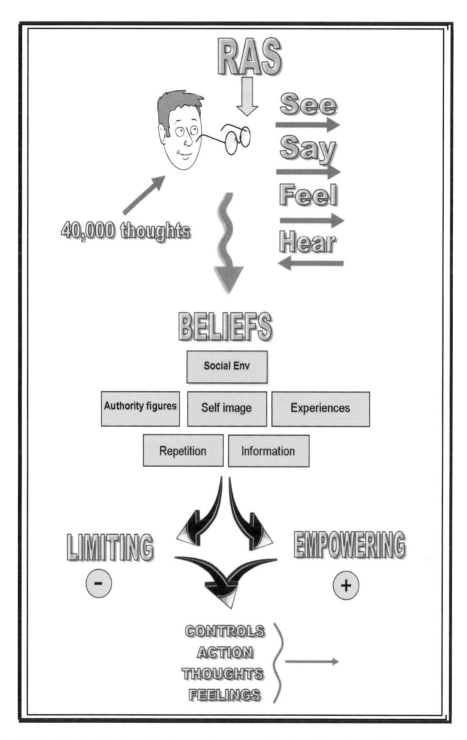

RAS = Reticular Activating System – how our brains take in and process what we see!

These are two simple examples, and you can see how these patterns can create a continuous circle of limiting or restricting actions. These patterns that validate the limiting beliefs, phrases and actions prevent progress forward. They will, unless we take notice of the situation, and take steps to 'break out' of this negative groove, remain self-perpetuating. This can seriously affect the progress towards achieving your goals!

> **The great thing in this world is not so much where we are, but in what direction we are moving**
>
> *Oliver Wendall Holmes*

This is a little bit of a mind teaser which is why I have covered this subject to break it down and 'peel the onion'. You can see the pattern and the fear of what can happen to create limiting actions and behaviours or indeed the opposite - the power to take empowering actions and take control!

NOTES:

Chapter 3 Summary

So you can see how there is a pattern which emerges between our beliefs, our use of words and a translation into our actions, which, in effect, shapes our behaviour. We have the power of changing these self-limiting patterns, indeed eradicating or avoiding them, as long as we can spot them. Knowing what they look, feel, sound and even smell like and where they came from is the key. Now let's have a look at some internal battles that go on within each of us every waking hour of the day.

'I am working every minute of the day to live positively and productively.'

Taken from Nick Owen "The Magic of Metaphor"
Primary source: Eleonara Gilbert
General Source: Native American Tradition

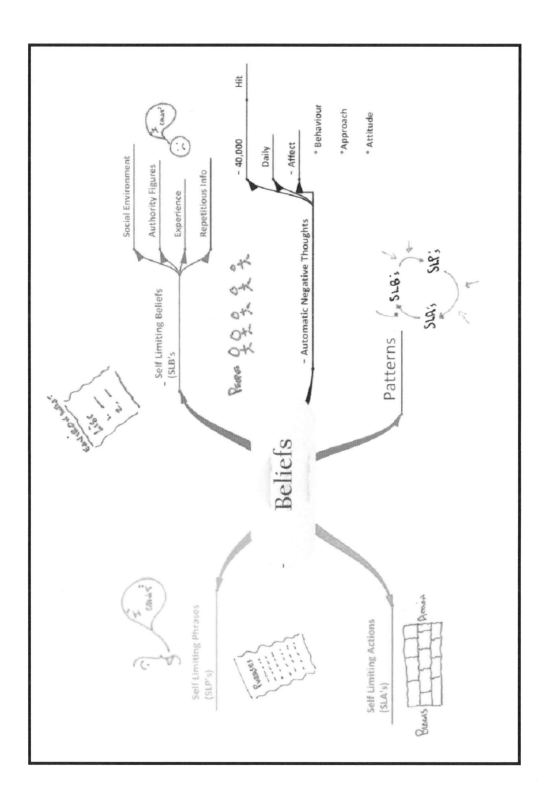

Chapter 4
Green Dragons vs White Knights

> He who is not courageous enough to take risks will accomplish nothing in life.
>
> *Muhammed Ali*

A glimpse at:-
- Automatic negative thoughts
- Understand / train / support / confidence
- Competence / incompetence / skills
- The reality of Fear

At the base of chapter 3 the story running through it is one of my favourites and I call it 'Dances with Wolves'. You may wish to read this story again before you start this chapter. A key message is that you have two voices or we have an internal battle between two forces. The negative forces of the 'Green Dragons' and the positive force of the 'White Knights'.

So you have 2 armies:

Green Dragons	White Knights
Fear	Peace
Greed	Love
Hatred	Kindness
Anger	Joy
Envy	Truth
False Pride	Compassion
Self-pity	Humility
Resentment	Transparency
Guilt	Authenticity
Inferiority	Friendship
Arrogance	Respect
Deceitfulness	Integrity
Superiority	Generosity
Selfishness	Benevolence
Jealousy	Faith
Conniving	Sharing
Dishonesty	Serenity
Boastfulness	Empathy

Which one will win?

"Whichever one you feed" is the answer! I am convinced that the hardest work we ever have to do to stay on top is to feed the White Knights and starve the Green Dragons. There are many methods but 'Affirmations' is my favourite.

Every time you anchor a positive affirmation into your mind you starve more Green Dragons and they cannot live without food.

The Green Dragons will <u>always</u> return but eventually they will become weaker and weaker. It takes time; sometimes you will be ambushed and sometimes they will sneak up on you in the dead of the night!

But, if you keep your White Knights uppermost in your mind with reserves in your sub-conscious – YOU WILL WIN!

So let's have a look at where you stand in the Green Dragons / White Knights battle:

The exercise below allows you to grade which Green Dragons pop up the most. There are 14 to choose from so take the 5 that you feel are the most prevalent on your 'mental stage' and put them in order of regularity. If you have any others that come up for you then add them to the list also.

> **Man is only truly great when he acts from his passions.**
>
> *Disraeli*

NOTES:

'I am embracing new challenges with an open heart and an open mind.'

Mountain Path

As I walked down the mountain path one day I happened upon an old lady, (or I thought she was an old lady).

1. Fear
2. Greed
3. Hatred
4. Anger
5. Envy
6. False Pride
7. Self-pity
8. Resentment
9. Guilt
10. Inferiority
11. Arrogance
12. Deceitfulness
13. Superiority
14. Selfishness
15. Boastfulness

TOP 5 FOR YOU

1. _____
2. _____
3. _____
4. _____
5. _____

> **Things that matter most, must never be at the mercy of things that matter least.**
>
> *Johann Wolfgang Von Goethe*

I could be wrong but in many people FEAR will appear in the top 5. It may even hold the No.1 spot. Before we look at this let's just take a minute to grade our White Knights too (again add any others that come up for you):

1. Peace
2. Love
3. Kindness
4. Joy
5. Truth
6. Compassion
7. Humility
8. Transparency
9. Authenticity
10. Friendship
11. Respect

TOP 5 FOR YOU

1. _____
2. _____
3. _____
4. _____
5. _____

NOTES:

'I am able to command and control the way I handle situations.'

She was struggling to get up the hill to the next village and carried with her a huge rucksack. I had not long left the village and so I offered to help her by carrying her rucksack for her.

12. Integrity
13. Generosity
14. Benevolence
15. Faith
16. Sharing
17. Serenity
18. Empathy

We now have our top 5 dragons and our top 5 knights, lets look at one of the dragons that I suspect comes into the major league for most people, FEAR, if it's not in your top 5 I might challenge your self-assessment! If it's there, then let's 'peel the onion' and find out what makes up this fear:

Is it a fear of something or some-one; a fear of a definite outcome or a possible outcome; are the dangers real or perceived?

NOTES:

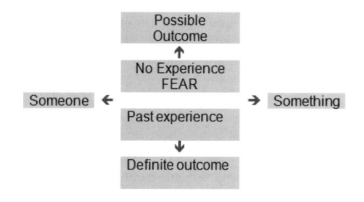

'I am consistently in control of how I conduct myself every day.'

The lady scowled at me and so I made sure that she understood my offer of help. I was in France and my French is good but something may have been lost in translation. So I repeated my offer.

It is this sort of reality checking or balance checking that can be carried out to test if this fear can be trusted indeed 'listened to'. What does this fear look like? To answer this we can break it down into 4 segments:

Physiological	Psychological
Behavioural	Emotional

We have all heard stories of people 'quaking in their boots' from a fearful situation thereby exhibiting a physiological and behavioural expression of fear.

We have also heard stories of actors 'freezing' on stage and suffering stage fright which is an experience of psychological and emotional fear.

So how do we overcome fear?

It goes without saying really but some fears are actually very real, installed by our biological control systems and our conditioning. For example the fear of fire; we know we shouldn't walk into a raging inferno unprotected due to the inevitable consequences of being burned to death. However members of the fire service with the correct protection and training along with the right back up and support can enter the same situation with a much lower risk-factor.

The outcome may still be injury or even death, but it is a 'considered risk' for the benefit of others and the fire

> All that we are is the result of what we have thought. The mind is everything. What we think we become.
>
> *The Buddha*

NOTES:

'I am constantly aware that I am a good person.'

She swore back at me in French and this time there was no misunderstanding, she was refusing help.

fighter has made a logical decision to take action based on the risk-factors involved.

It is interesting to consider the logical steps that the fire-fighter goes through in order to reach his decision:

I am about to walk into a burning building which is ablaze with flames

↓

Logic says – **I should not do this**

↓

Past Conditioning says – **The flames and fire are dangerous**

↓

Recent Training and Conditioning says –
I can wear protective clothing
I have been trained to deal with this
(This shows understanding and knowledge)
I trust my team
I trust my superior to not place me in danger
(This shows trust and support)
I have done this before and I was OK
(This shows confidence through practice)
I am doing this for a good reason (to protect or save a life)
(This shows the motivation for the action)

This is a very simplistic scenario, but with some very interesting aspects. We have a fire fighter who, prior to being trained and part of a team, would not have entered that house while it was on fire, but with the right mind set, the correct training and all the support

> **Some men see things as they are, and say, why? I dream of things that never were, I say, why not?**
>
> *George Bernard Shaw*

NOTES:

'I am constantly aware of my positive attributes.'

I understood and considered this situation. She could have been proud and therefore not willing to accept help.

of his team, along with the right motivation and his own solid affirmations, was able to enter the building with confidence and rescue those trapped there without doing any damage to himself.

I wonder if we can apply this to some other fears which may not be so real or obvious. Let's look at the steps again:

> There is no such thing in anyone's life as an unimportant day.
>
> *Alexander Woolcott*

Past life experiences tell you not to do it!		
Understanding	U	He/She has a grasp and understanding of the fear factor of the given situation
Training	T	He/She has been trained to understand the risks involved and how to be safe or avoid the risks
Support	S	He/She has the right support team around him/her
Confidence	C	He/She has the confidence to proceed
Motivation	M	He/She has the right motivation to proceed and succeed

NOTES:

'I am capable of handling all situations positively.'

She may have been afraid of strangers albeit I consider myself to be "friendly and un–scary" in nature.

Mmm... This looks like a plan to overcome quite a few fears and barriers that stand in our way! This could be a little bit of 'methodology' to help us walk though the fear barrier. **But don't forget the 'WHY' has to be strong.**

For every decision we make there is a subconscious decision tree we follow and the key to progressing forward is to interfere with the decision tree and bring into the world a NEW YOU!!

> I don't want to get to the end of my life and find that I lived just the length of it. I want to have lived the width of it as well.
>
> *Diane Ackerman*

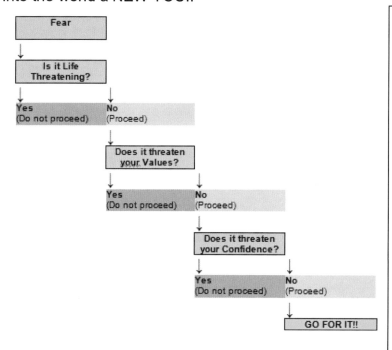

NOTES:

So there we have it, we have fear with its basic dichotomy - fear of harm or danger and the suppressed natural fight or flight physical responses available.

Everything is happening perfectly and according to plan.

She could have been a bit grumpy or have number of reasons for refusing help.

We have the question posed which is whether this fear is instinctive or conditional and we have the fear of harm or danger to our emotional or mental equilibrium, which is again instinctive or conditional.

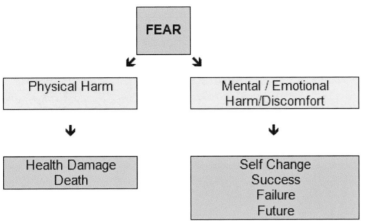

We set this against the background of the cognitive systems as laid out by R.Thailer and C. Sunstein in their book 'NUDGE' where they suggest that we have 2 cognitive systems; automatic and reflective

A= Automatic	R= Reflective
Uncontrolled	Controlled
Effortless	Effortful
Associative	Deductive
Fast	Slow
Unconscious	Self-Aware
Skilled	Rule following

This also falls very much in line with what Malcolm Gladwell talks about in his book 'BLINK'. He calls it instinctive thinking or deliberate thinking. Whatever

You will either step forward into GROWTH, or you will step back into safety.

Abraham Maslow

NOTES:

'I am in total control of what I think, feel and do.'

She was resting and still a little animated and so determined to get to the bottom of this I sat down and waited for her to calm down. She did calm down and I offered to help for the third time, clearly, calmly and kindly.

97

you call it the same rule applies. According to my thinking this is that regardless of how we got to where we are today, the Automatic and Reflective cognitive systems and our instinctive or deliberate thinking styles shape the way we react and think. This is regardless of whether or not our current processing system is the result of our biologically evolved mental state. The key when we look at fear is to take some tools and methods to combat it, indeed, who is to say that with the right methods and motivations we can't re-programme ourselves to take a fear and recondition our minds into changing the way we respond to it in order to overcome it, or better, not even feel it in the first place.

Alternatively we can look at how we actually tune our reactions to a mental or emotional fear from reflective to automatic and from deliberate to instinctive. How on earth do we do this? Hard work, I'm afraid. We need to go back to basics and work on each element of our thinking. But just think, how wonderful it would be to live life without fear! Well worth the effort required.

Look at the learning model below for a great many skills we take for granted in life:

The classic example of this is the baby that starts to crawl and is quite happy crawling as now it can get about. All around it people are showing that the role model for human beings is that they walk. Originally the baby had no idea that it was meant to walk and didn't know that there were other skills that it didn't yet know (it was a subconscious incompetent). It began

Living is easy with your eyes closed, misunder-standing all you see.

John Lennon

NOTES:

'I am aware all the time that every minute of my life must be cherished and enjoyed.'

At which point she burst into tears and wept and wept for what seemed ages.

to see grown ups all around it walking, running and generally getting around, so it began to try (it was a conscious incompetent). The grown ups would push, prompt and encourage the baby to try to walk, but it didn't know how and would keep tumbling and bashing into things. Slowly and with help it cautiously put one foot in front of the other and kept trying until it had mastered the art, (it was a conscious competent), and of course now the baby is walking and running without even thinking about it, (it is a subconscious competent).

> **You must become what you want to attract. Be the kind of person you would want to surround yourself with.**
>
> *Susan Jeffers*

NOTES:

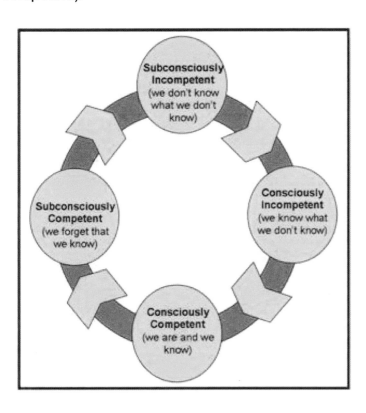

'There is no security in life, but there is opportunity'

I was in no rush and whilst I like to help people in life I certainly don't like causing them stress. I waited and eventually asked how on earth I had caused so much anger, indignation and then upset.

We then forget that we have had to learn these skills literally step by step. If you were to stop a 10 year old in the street and ask him to explain how to walk you would more than likely get a very strange reaction. Everyone knows how to walk right? It just comes naturally! Well you know that it doesn't. Everything we do without thinking about it has to be learned in the first instance. We can therefore learn anything and practise and practise until we can do it without thinking about it! We can even overcome fear in this way. We take small steps, we tumble, we cry, we get cuddles and reassurance from our role models until finally we master the skill.

So, back to the mental and emotional fears: Success, Failure, Change, Self, Future. We need to take a long hard look at where we are on the fear scale and establish what tiny steps we can take to move towards becoming unconsciously competent at dealing with those fears. We go back to our toolbox and we use:

- Affirmations
- Visualisations
- Clarity of Purpose
- Motivation
- Goals
- Support
- Mentors
- Role Models
- Practice - individual or coached
- Feedback - internal or external

> **We must overcome the notion that we must be ordinary ... it robs you of the chance to be extraordinary and leads you to the mediocre.**
>
> *Uta Hagen*

NOTES:

'If you do nothing, nothing happens!'

She responded very strongly and began to take out the stones that she carried in the ruck sack. This stone is for the child I lost at child birth.

Within reason there should be no mental or emotional fear that you cannot overcome. Good luck! Let's move forward together and get this cracked!

Chapter 4 Summary

So you have been bold enough to face up to some gremlins, demons, Green Dragons (fears) and stare them right in the eye. You have identified your White Knights and realised the balance between positive and negative mind games.

You have seen how fear can be justified and unjustified, real and un-real, valid and un-validated. The skill is to understand, to overcome and to master. The action you must take is to practice this understanding regularly. Now let's move to one of my favourite methods of fending off the Dragons - Affirmations.

> **Other people have lots of plans for you – but passion and authenticity will find you freedom and power. It takes courage to do what you want.**
>
> *Susan Sarandon*

NOTES:

'I am focused on achieving little changes to my life with simple steps.'

This is the stone for when I lost my job at the mill, this is the stone for when our roof was blown off in the storm, this is the stone for the heart murmur I have, this is the stone for my son who does not speak to me, and she went on unloading! She insisted that she always had to carry this load!

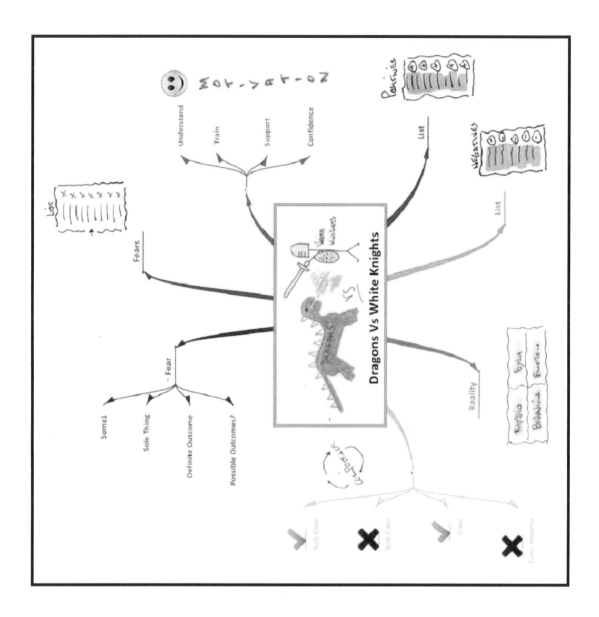

Dragons Vs White Knights

Chapter 5
Positive Affirmations

A glimpse at:-

- Affirmations
- Ten tips
- Linking to goals
- Regular usage

Faith is the ability to see the invisible and believe in the incredible and that is what enables believers to receive what the masses think is impossible.

Clarence Smithson

NOTES:

One of my favourite stories is the *'Dancing with Wolves'* story which you read in Chapter 3. It really is one of my favourite stories because it tends to extrapolate so many things that I see when coaching and guiding individuals to find their 'true path', their 'true purpose' or empowering them towards achieving their goals. The parallel I see is the battle between the *'Green Dragons and White Knights'* (Chapter 4). In essence one way to look at this is the conflict between self-limiting beliefs and the quest for progress, underpinned by one of my success habits (pages 30-33) with positive objectives. Positive objectives can come from your goals and aspirations or indeed your true purpose or single list of SLBs (Self-Limiting Beliefs) that you are trying hard to remove or bypass which are often buried deep in your subconscious.

I am confident and certain of my ability to achieve what I choose.

Sailing Towards Goals

Not long ago I was invited to sail the Solent by a good friend of mine and went off for a group sail with 5-6 friends in a beautiful purpose built yacht called a Bristol Pilot.

There are a few rules with setting out affirmations, so let us look back at these. For me, the rules are as follows. They should:

1. Be *stated out aloud*.
2. Be stated in the *first person*.
3. Use *power phrases*
4. *Resonate* with you and linked to your goals.
5. Be *moving forward phrases* not *away from* phrases.
6. Be *looked at regularly*.
7. Be *written out* on cards that can be easily carried around (or on your smart phone).
8. Be *recorded* to non-lyrical music (ideally evocative and powerful).
9. Be *collective*, so put together in a series e.g. five to ten per goal.
10. Be *everlasting* and not limited to time (unless you require them to be linked with a time-sensitive goal).

Goal linking is great fun and very empowering as it helps you to bring your life in synergy with your goals. It makes them come alive, serving as a constant reminder of what you truly want to achieve. There are going to be those whose thoughts argue that we will regularly implode, go through a 'relapse' back to our 'old ways', if we do not deal with our Self-Limiting Beliefs first, then go about setting our positive thought process. I strongly disagree with this argument. I believe that the affirmations can kick-start the process by which those SLBs will be gradually replaced by positive self-beliefs! Initially start by saying the affirmations out loud, there may be a natural conflict

Stop doubting and believe.

John 21:27

NOTES:

I know I am capable of anything I wish to achieve.

I had only ever sailed once and so the excitement was high as we set off on the first day heading out to sea.

with our own thoughts. How can I say this when I do not believe it? But, the brain is a marvellous machine that is open to positive brain-washing as much as negative brain-washing! Will this game of push me– pull you last forever? I actually believe it goes all the way back to the *'Dancing with Wolves'* story – which ever you feed the most wins!

Lets face it if we believe what we are told, we have 40,000 thoughts *attacking* us every day; there is a lot of work to do. Let's take the hypothesis that our world goes from – 'you can do anything you want to do' which is an empowering phase that parents should be saying to their children to engender an aspirational and positive mind set in them. Then start to look at what age 'limiting' starts the 'do not do that because'. I am genuinely not sure in my case, so let's say around the age of 11 when I went off to boarding school. The age will be different for everyone and will also be dependent on our parents, our environment and our upbringing (nature vs nurture). As the ink is drying on this manuscript I am 52 years old so let's do the maths on these A.N.T.S. (Automatic Negative Thoughts)

> 52 years - 11 = 41yrs x 365 days
> = 14,695 days x 40,000 thoughts
> **= 598,000,000 thoughts**

Wow! This is quite a battle 598 million Self-Limiting Beliefs have floated past our thoughts and to a certain extent shaped our actions or should I say my actions for the last 41 years!

> **The best thing about the future is that is comes only one day at a time.**
>
> **Abraham Lincoln**

NOTES:

Everything I do is effortless and happening perfectly.

We hit what seemed to be a period of serious hard work as we set about tacking. Lots of hard work and lots of physical exercise going back and forth against the wind and the tide. Hardly moving towards our destination at all.

No wonder it is a hard journey to take to build a life into a positive lifestyle, into a life where we trust in our ability, into a life where we adopt possibility thinking! Do I believe we have to develop a Self Limiting Phrase-watching process (SLP), as in, do I have to go through 598 million positive affirmations to negate or stop the A.N.T.S? We can start with the regular use of positive affirmations, said out loud with power, strength and passion which will certainly help the process.

In essence it is a structured way to reintroduce some White Knights into the subconscious as the day begins, and patience to fight against the Green Dragons. Without wanting to leave on a negative, I suggest that these S.L.B's (Self-Limiting Beliefs) or Green Dragons are never far away. For me my most vulnerable times are when I am tired. I really do need to watch for the Green Dragons or self limiting beliefs attacking me in these moments. Do you know when you are at your strongest and your weakest?

What works for me is speaking affirmations in the morning to start the day, with a reminder of who I am and where I stand. I guess it is bringing the White Knights to order to help me in my day. That is my visualisation, but you will need to seek your own picture or feeling as to how they can be best brought to life. I visualise two things - White Knights are the positive thoughts in my head, Green Dragons are the negative thoughts in my head.

The other thing I do is to practice the verbal 'hands off' which is to actually recognise when I am being

> I've discovered that numerous peak performers use the skill of mental rehearsal of visualisation. They mentally run through important events before they happen.
>
> *Charles Garfield*

NOTES:

I make good decisions that benefit me and others.

Every twenty minutes a flurry of activity and "coming about"!

This tacking phase went on for 2-3 hours and the morale of some of the crew seemed to dampen somewhat.

attacked by the S.L.B's and openly state some form of sentence "I am not listening to you guys!" I then launch into one or two positive affirmations. This can happen at anytime of the day. Mind you, in this society of ours you might need to be careful of where your tendency to conduct this self-talk should be, driven by exactly where you are physically! It might be nice to do some muttering under your breath if you are in a queue in your local supermarket or travelling on the tube or train as a commuter. People may not understand! That is of course not your problem, but I am also a great believer in politeness and good manners, linked to a respect of other people's personal space.

Ok, you have become used to the way I work and the way that I guide my clients or people who need my support. So, will you actually put this into practise? Make a decision? Will you use the affirmation method? Tick the relevant boxes:

> To empower my existing goals. ☐
> To fight against my S.L.B.'s. ☐
> To underpin my prime purpose*. ☐
> I will not try this method. ☐

* Some people have one driving aim they are working on, some have several aims. So your prime purpose may be one or several significant goals you are heading for.

If you do not want to try this method that is absolutely fine by the way. No offence taken!

> **There are no secrets to success. It is the result of preparation, hard work, and learning from failure.**
>
> *Colin L Powell*

NOTES:

I have choice and always make good choices that bring me fulfillment and happiness.

I personally was quite happy with the whole ritual and had no idea whether we were making good time to Yarmouth or not! But some of the others were less than happy.

Just a reminder of your top ten goals, just jot them down here:

	What?	By When?
1		
2		
3		
4		
5		
6		
7		
8		
9		
10		

The destiny of man is in his own soul.

Heroclotus

Now simply try putting together a sentence while following the rules I gave you on page 103, for each of the goals.

So linking the goals:

1. I am ...
2.
3.
4.
5.
6.
7.
8.
9.
10.

NOTES:

I have an example: My goal is to swim the BT Swimathon this year. So I am saying "I am swimming the 5000m swim for charity with ease this year."

I see problems as seeds of opportunity.

As if by some miracle everything changed and the tacking stopped and the wind was behind us and we started hurtling along at some considerable speed. We were now covering distances that previously we had to attack with massive amounts of energy but moving at an indiscernible snail's pace.

My own personal experience is that the use of just one sentence of affirmations per goal is not really enough to focus the mind truly in the right direction. I would therefore recommend that you do a series of affirmations for each goal, perhaps five or possibly even 10. I write these on index cards and rotate which ones I read each day, either by choice, or by virtue of the fact that I am only focusing on a particular goal that day/week. But at least we have had a look at them and kept the White Knights to the fore. Simply reflect upon them as and when appropriate. You can get ideas from the affirmation CD I have recorded. However, the *'piece de resistance'* is to write them yourself, and then maybe record them on your phone or computer. My readings are just a prompt, or an indication of what can be done.

With the S.L.B's or Green Dragons battle this is a little distracting or draining, but let's have a go! Can you list ten of the S.L.B's that pop into your mind on a regular basis? Try it by starting with a classic series of those S.L.B words.

1. I can't….!
2. I can never…..!
3. I always…..!
4. I wish I could…..!
5. I never seem to…..!
6. If only I could….!
7. Why do other people…..!
8. It's not that, it's because…….!
9. They don't understand because……!
10. I can try but……..!

> **You must be resolutely determined that whatever you do shall always be the best of which you are capable.**
>
> *Charles E Popplestone*

NOTES:

I strive to find the answers to challenges.

We covered the 15 -16 miles left of our journey in no time at all and the ease with which we ploughed through the waves was exhilarating to say the least. Effort involved? None at all. I wonder if this is the way working at our goals sometimes takes shape. We work hard, we put the effort in.

Now take the 10 S.L.B's and let's knock down these dragons with some affirmations using the same technique as before match the affirmations to the S.L.B, this your future armour and shield to be used at all times!

1. I am ….
2. I can….
3. I will
4. ....
5. ......
6. ....
7. .....
8. ......
9. ......
10. ....

I promise you this, you will be shocked by the change in your attitude as you play this game. With affirmations to underpin your Prime Purpose this is a similar method to the goal linking. However, you could also try this little technique which I have used. You write out on one page of A4 ten to twenty sentences describing what you are doing now that you have achieved your Prime Purpose. Where will you be?
Who will you be with? What will you be doing? Make it real, make it poetic, make it descriptive.

THEN, find a piece of music, (no lyrics), and create your picture with the music. Make sure you talk out loud, slowly, calmly and wait to feel the tingle down your spine. If your spine is tingling you have locked into the right purpose or close to it.

> **Life is a succession of moments. To live each one is to succeed.**
>
> *Conita Kent*

NOTES:

I am part of the universe and open to its power, energy and information.

We do all the things the books tell us to. We focus, we affirm and we put in so much effort - enough to make ourselves weep - with seemingly no change, no results and no reward. Then suddenly we are full steam (sail) ahead with progress being made and success being achieved at break-neck speed.

So...

How do we make this habit of affirmations into an integral part of our life? Well with the magic of computers these days, one thing you can use to make it easy to lay out our own accountability checks in an Excel spreadsheet, or maybe just jot it down in your diary.

> Every positive change – every jump to a higher level of energy and awareness involves a rite of passage … we must go through a period of discomfort, of initiation.
> *Dan Millman*

So there you have it. We know how to battle against S.L.B's or Green Dragons and how to harness the power of affirmations to start the fight against the years and years of A.N.T.s attacking us. As we move forward to affirm and achieve our short, medium and long term goals, our life becomes its own positive affirmation that we can achieve, we can succeed and we can be masters of our own direction. We do have the power to take control. We do have the opportunity to change what is and certainly have the ability to negotiate with the negative message and limiting beliefs.

NOTES:

Excel Example Chart – Affirmations Done?

	Mon	Tues	Wed	Thurs	Fri	Sat	Sun
Week 1	✓	✓	✓	✓	✓	✓	✓
Week 2	✓	✗	✓	✓	✗	✓	✓
Week 3	✓	✓	✗	✓	✓	✓	✓
Week 4	✓	✗	✓	✓	✓	✓	✗

I let the universe know what I want and leave the details to the universe.

The skipper knew what would happen but us novices had no idea and were sometimes too shy to ask. Will it be OK?

Another way to reinforce your affirmations and positive thoughts is to create a 'dreamboard' with images of your goals and dreams (see page 113). You can hang this up in a prominent place as a constant reminder of your destination. It is fun to create and it is surprising how seeing this each day will help your mind to accept what you are working towards.

> **Have the courage to be yourself. The courage to be unique.**
>
> *Salma Hayek*

Some of my Affirmations Cards

I pay attention to those things I wish to improve.

I wonder if this is like achieving all goals and I wonder if the use of faith in ourselves, faith in our own journey and faith in our path. (often tested to the hilt), is the key.

Chapter 5 Summary

So we have looked at Affirmations, one of my favourite methodologies both for myself and for my coaching clients to embed positive thoughts into the mind. How to develop a 'Star Trek' mental force-field around your mind and body to build up your resistance to the negative daily bombardment of life. This is one success habit I would recommend you adopt with gusto. Try it, review it and apply it. It works! Now let's look at goals and it is the power of positive affirmations linked to goals which is, in my opinion, a force to be reckoned with.

One of my Dreamboards

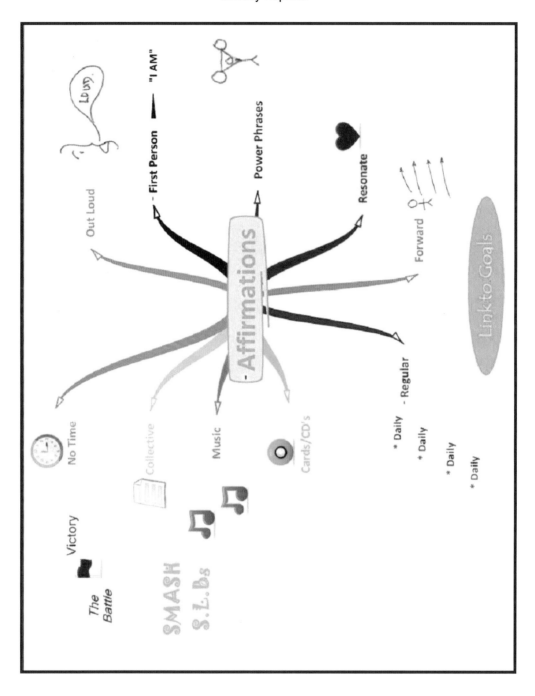

Chapter 6
Goals, Intentions, Dreams

A glimpse at:-

- Goals
- Steps
- Structure
- Monitoring
- Values

> **Having a dream isn't stupid. It's not having one that's stupid.**
>
> *Cliff Clavin (Cheers)*

NOTES:

For me a goal is something that you want to achieve but it has some particular aspects. Thousands of books and papers have been written on the subject to help guide people as to the crafting of their goals. I don't believe there is a right or wrong way to plan goals and in fact the key is to have them!

So, however you get to write down your goals is the right way.

A goal is an intention or a destination which is specific, measurable, achievable, realistic and there is a time line to it – S.M.A.R.T.

I have my own particular method for crafting goals in my goal journal.

'I am continually stretching myself towards my goals.'

Simon

There was a boy named Simon whose family brought him up well with solid values and clear guidelines for life. They always said to him at the start of the day "You are a good person, you have a beautiful heart and the world will

You will all have your own goals but to jump ahead a little let's just jot down your top ten goals which are likely to span across these areas:

1. Family
2. Relationships
3. Finances
4. Career
5. Business
6. Community
7. Health
8. Social Life
9. Personal Development
10. Education/Learning
11. Spiritual
12. Life Purpose

> **If you don't daydream and plan things out in your imagination, you never get there. So you have to start somewhere.**
> *Robert Duvall*

NOTES:

	What	What area it involves	By when	Short/Medium/Long
Example	Lose ½ stone	Health	1st April this year	Short Term
1				
2				
3				
4				
5				
6				
7				
8				
9				
10				

OK, so why do things sometimes go wrong? Or what are the key things I have seen Distort or Disturb the process of goal setting for the 1000's of clients I have worked with over the last few years?

'I am creating my own life, my way, in line with my goals.'

always be good to you when you hold this to be true.".

This statement was affirmed to him every day for the first seventeen years of his life without fail.

1. The goal has no <u>measurability</u> or is not specific enough.
2. Things get <u>in the way.</u>
3. The goal has not been crafted in <u>synergy with personal values.</u>
4. The reality of the <u>timeline</u> is wrong.

> **Happiness lies in the joy of achievement and of creative effort.**
>
> *Franklin Roosevelt*

Let's look at these in turn. An awareness of what can go wrong is essential, because if the wrong goal is crafted, the lack of its achievement can cause GOAL CONFIDENCE BREAKDOWN. I have experienced this and I will confess that as a result I lacked the confidence to craft good ones for a period of at least 5 years. Why?

NOTES:

The goal has no measurability

I am always aware that there is a difference between what I call hard and soft goals. Hard goals are specific and they are very easy to define with the key question of 'how much of what, by when?'

E.g. I will lose 1 stone in weight by the 1st April this year.

This is what I call a hard goal, not due to the fact that losing weight for some is difficult. But by the sheer fact that there are one-way clear strategy posts that can be set for this goal:-

- Where are you now? – what weight?
- How long do we have? – let's say 3 months
- How will you do it? – let's say by the removal of carbohydrates in the diet!

> *'I am forging forward towards my goals every single day of my life.'*

Simon sadly got caught up with a "bad crowd" for a while, involving himself in minor crime and some wild activities and from time to time the group he was in fell out and the altercations that ensued were unpleasant and possibly drug-induced.

We can then structure staging posts or what I call success signposts along the way.

We may decide to do a weigh-in every week and then chart our success diary this way:

	Date	Weight Now
Start		
1.		
2.		
3.		
4.		
5.		
6.		
7.		
8.		
9.		
10.		
11.		
12.		
End		

1. Why? – to feel better about myself.
2. How? – Low Carb diet. Lets look at my goal of setting up a low carb diet and the elements to it. I call this 'peeling the onion' and putting teeth and support around the goal. Making it come alive, encouraging help and support to ensure its success.
3. Success signposts – weekly weigh in.
4. What could get in the way? – I used to love pasta!
5. What will help? – clever intensive diet.

> **I play the odds – the harder I work the more likely I am to succeed.**
>
> *Jonny Wilkinson*

NOTES:

'I am consistently working on achieving my goals.'

Police cautions were involved and lots of soul-searching was done by Simon and his parents who stood by their values and whilst disappointed by their son's behaviour never lost sight of their love for him and made him well aware of this.

6. Who will help? – partner will do the same.
7. Celebration – buy a new suit at new size.
8. Accountability – tell all my friends.
9. Does it match up to your values?

You can see from this specific hard goal the classic steps required:-

1. What do you want?
2. By when?
3. Why?
4. How will you do this?
5. How often will you measure progress?
6. How will you make yourself accountable?
7. What might get in the way?
8. What will help you?
9. Who will help you?
10. How will you celebrate?
11. Does the goal match your values?

So what if you have a 'soft' goal – e.g. spend more time with my family?

How on earth do you approach that one?

Well to be fair the best thing to do here is simply to 'peel the onion' a little bit more. This is appropriate where you come across, or find yourself using, terms like – 'more than', 'less than', 'reduce', 'lessen'. The key is simply to define the 'more than' or define the 'less than'. If I take the example of the 'spend more time with my family' we simply need to challenge our own goal and ask 'what do you mean by *more*?'

> **Dream BIG dreams. Set BIG goals. Expect a miracle – because that is exactly what you are.**
>
> *Peter Field*

NOTES:

'I am crafting my goals on a regular basis.'

At some stage his father even said "Son, you must be aware that I will always love you but I don't like you as a person right now."

When I have worked with individuals in the past we simply look back at the past and consider where this goal comes from and look at 'more than' what? We identify the number of hours, days or weeks that are currently being spent with the family (in this case). We can then decide our aims as in 'where are we now'? From here we can define what 'more than' means and exactly how much more time you want to spend with them. Is this figure realistic? How will you achieve this?

So there you have it, no matter how fluffy the goal may be, (albeit the intention is sound and honorable), we can, with a little bit of thought, break it down into definable aspects so that we can measure it.

Things getting in the way?

Goal achievement = Success – How you deal with interruptions and interference?

In reality the interruptions and interference give us a number of things to consider. Have a think about a goal that you may have set and missed. Why don't you reflect upon your possible reasons for missing it?

1. Fear of success   Yes/No
2. Self-sabotage   Yes/No
3. Lack of self confidence   Yes/No
4. Self condemnation   Yes/No
5. Poor concentration   Yes/No
6. Trying too hard   Yes/No

> **Enjoy the little things, for one day you may look back and realise they were the big things.**
>
> *Robert Brautt*

NOTES:

I know I can achieve my goals.

Simon plunged into the normal spiral swept along by his peer group. His past values became clouded and pushed along by his desire to be accepted by his mates his life was becoming controlled by the lowest common denominator, the "peer group" pressure.

7. Lack of will power	Yes/No
8. Being a perfectionist	Yes/No
9. A different priority pushed it away	Yes/No
10. Overwhelm	Yes/No

> There is so much in the world for us all if we only have the eyes to see it, and the heart to love it, and the hand to gather it ourselves ...
> *Lucy Maud Montgomery*

The key with missing a goal is the awareness of the potential problems standing in the way. The 10 reasons mentioned here are deep subjects in themselves to be considered at length by you and your coach, mentor or partner or whoever is helping you achieve your goals. Where these interruptions take their place is the 'potential obstacle' section of the goal setting process. Have a good look at what has happened before. Here are a few guidelines for you, I am not suggesting for one second this is easy but the guidelines will perhaps help you to think through how you may be able to overcome these interruptions or interferences.

- FEAR OF SUCCESS
  Ask yourself the question "what are you afraid of"? Take the fear apart, walk around it; what is worst that can happen?

- SELF-SABOTAGE
  Have a good look at this. Think about what made you pull the plug! Think about the possible reasons. Could this have been the wrong goal?

NOTES:

My goals are in line with my purpose in life.

Things became rather bad for a while and Simon began to hate himself and also lost sight of all the good things in life he used to stand for. He even started to believe his parents would disown him and no longer loved him.

- LACK OF SELF-CONFIDENCE
  Self-confidence can be built by what I call 'baby steps'; a little bit at a time. The goal may have been too big all at once.

- SELF-CONDEMNATION
  This stems from the A.N.T.S discussed in early chapters. The whole key is to move forward and not to look back.

- POOR CONCENTRATION
  This can be helped by regular reminders of the goal, daily mind-joggers, visible reminders, and the participation of helpers, partners and colleagues.

- TRYING TOO HARD
  Too much effort can actually be just like fitness training and doing too much too soon. Could it be taken slower? Could you extend the timescale?

- LACK OF WILLPOWER
  Willpower can be learned and dumbed down. Is/was the *why* strong enough? The reason/vision must be powerful enough to drive you.

- BEING A PERFECTIONIST
  Ask yourself the question, when *will* it be enough? The issue with perfection is that one never gets there!

> **The poor man is not he who is without cent, but he who is without a dream.**
>
> *Harry Kemp*

NOTES:

I am excited about achieving my goals.

Confused and battered by social pressure he carried on his silly ways for a while. Waking up one morning in a police holding cell, unable to summon up the courage to ask his family for help, he wept and wept for hours.

- A DIFFERENT PRIORITY OVERTAKES IT
  Did the alternative priority deserve to be put in front of this goal? Was it the right thing to do? Did it actually make sense?

- OVERWHELM
  Was the goal too much? Was it too big? Was it realistic for the timescale?

- THE GOAL HAS NOT BEEN CRAFTED IN SYNERGY WITH YOUR VALUES
  This is quite a heavy one on the surface but actually it is simple to resolve! Go back to your goal journal and have a good look at your values. The goal must be in line with your values otherwise you simply will not have the necessary passion behind to fulfil it. How can you put this to the test? You may wish to list your *top ten values* and align them with your goals.

Values Exercise

Look at the list of words on the next two pages and try to highlight the 12 which resonate with you the most. What I mean by that is which words when you read them make you think "mmm I believe in that" or "mmm that word lives in my world".

Now once you have highlighted the 12, get a pen and list them in rank order, 1 being the most important value, 12 being the least important.

> **We have forty million reasons for failure but not a single excuse.**
>
> *Rudyard Kipling*

NOTES:

I know that I am capable of achieving my goals.

During this total hysteria of disgust with himself and complete abdication of his own responsibility, forgetting the real love that existed from his family, a voice came to him from his deep sub-conscious. It was a voice which he had heard for 365 days a year for the first 17 years of his life "you are a good person, …

Determination
Directness
Discipline
Education
Effort
Elegance
Empowerment
Enthusiasm
Equality
Excellence
Fairness
Focus
Forgiveness
Freedom
Friendliness
Fun
Financial Security
Family
Generosity
Happiness
Harmony
Health
Helpfulness
Honesty
Honour
Humility
Humour
Imagination
Independence
Individualism
Influence
Integrity
Intuition

Mercy
Morality
Modesty
Moderation
Obedience
Openness
Optimism
Order
Organisation
Patience
Partnership
Peace
Perfection
Perseverance
Personal Growth
Pleasure
Power
Prudence
Quality
Recognition
Respect
Responsibility
Risk-taking
Safety
Self-awareness
Self-reliance
Self-respect
Sensitivity
Sharing
Sincerity
Spirituality
Stability
Success...

> **The difference between perseverance and obstinacy is that the one often comes from a strong will, and the other from a strong won't.**
>
> *Henry Ward Beecher*

NOTES:

My goals are exciting and drive me to action.

You have a beautiful heart, and the world will be good to you when you hold this to be true."

Simon somehow snapped out of his mental "mist" used his free phone call.

Joy   Tact
Justice   Tenacity
Kindness   Tolerance
Learning   Tradition
Levity   Trust
Love   Wealth
Loyalty   Wisdom

> **One today is worth two tomorrows; never leave that till tomorrow which you can do today**
> *Benjamin Franklin*

There will be other words that come into your world which you may wish to add. This is not a finite list. The list is drawn from a variety of personal development books that I use.

So your top 12 values are:-

1.
2.
3.
4.
5.
6.
7.
8.
9.
10.
11.
12.

You will find something very spooky happens when you are considering your goals. If they match and are in alignment with your *values* they will happen. If they are not true to your values they are less likely to happen. Also when people ask you to help or get involved with something you can quite simply cross reference with your core values and make a decision

NOTES:

My goals will happen perfectly and according to plan.

He called his father and was immediately helped, without reservation by his family through the trials and tribulations of the legal world and given another chance. Simon never looked back from that moment. He gained a grant to set up a business which has grown from strength to strength and now turns over in

based on whether this task or project matches your values. It gives you a great strength to be able to say "yes" as well as saying "no".

Goals   Which 2-3 values match
                                   with this goal?

_____   _____

_____   _____

_____   _____

_____   _____

_____   _____

> **The intelligent man is one who has successfully fulfilled many accomplishments, and is yet willing to learn more**
>
> *Ed Parker*

NOTES:

This is the acid test. Ask your heart, does your goal feel in line with your values?

- THE REALITY OF THE TIMELINE IS WRONG! This also is less challenging than you might think. We always want the results to come a lot faster than possible. There can be an emotion that drives us to believe that anything and everything is possible, but the reality is that the bravery required to set and craft goals is significant. In essence we all live incredibly busy lives and so our noble efforts to change things are to be admired and regarded with a tremendous amount of pride.

The answer here, therefore, is potentially to give yourself a break! Have a long hard look at the timescale on each goal. If you were building a house

I am celebrating my successes.

Excess of £1m per annum. Funnily enough the corporate mantra which can be seen on every piece of marketing literature which his team produce is:-

We are good people. We have beautiful hearts.
We believe we are in the world to be good to you. Try us and find this to be true.

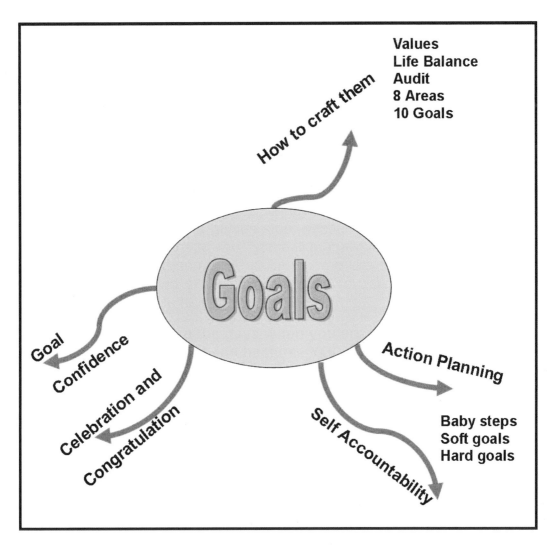

what would sit in the build plan? Contingency Funds? What else? Must we assume that we will over-run? So while are you crafting your goals, planning your goals analytically – give yourself a CHANCE TO <u>SUCCEED</u>!

Chapter 6 Summary

So the natural flow goes from establishing values to crafting goals across the whole spectrum of your world. This can be done on a short, medium and long-term basis. We have learned how to create bench-marks and sign-posts from the start of a goal to the end. Plus, we know how to review and monitor how the progress of a goal is going. All successful people write their goals down, review them and monitor them regularly. Next we are going to look at one way to grab back some control in your life.

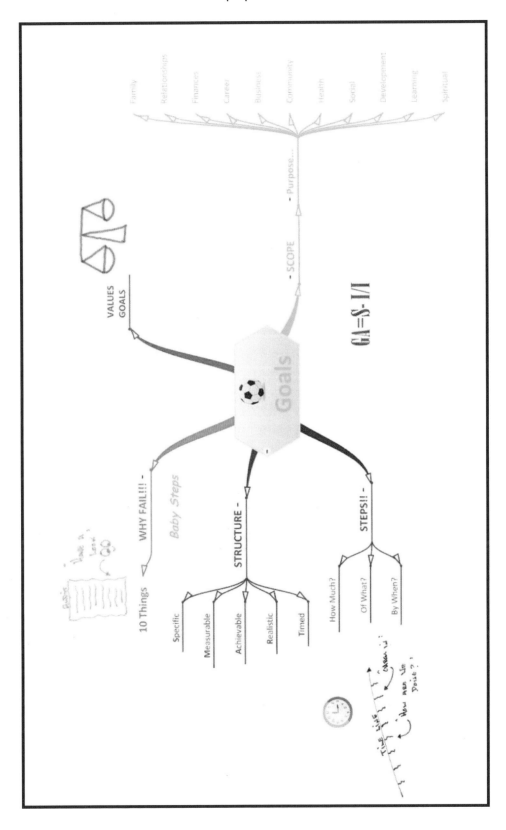

Chapter 7
Grab Back Your Life

A glimpse at:-

- The Maths behind your life
- Plan your weekend
- Plan your time
- Time plan linked to goals

NOTES:

I sometimes wonder about where we stand in the world of fear! Do we, in the main, plunge ourselves into a week, a month, a year and just 'get on with it'? Thus avoiding any confrontation with any fears, bypassing the chance to break new boundaries and truly stretch ourselves. Is it this immersion into a 'normal' life, which actually creates our inner armour and our protection against harm? Is it our safe zone and are we ultimately happy and content there? Or is that we have enclosed ourselves in a 'bubble' where we do not have to go through the mental pain of change and personal development?

To that end, I do recall through my own life seemingly losing weeks, months and possibly even years to the treadmill of life. The routine of Monday to Friday – the weekends starting on a Friday night, and attempting to break up the week with 'lily pads of happiness', which is the way my sister describes it. Have you ever

'I am taking strong, well considered steps to enjoying and cherishing my weekends.'

The frog in the well

There was once a frog stuck at the bottom of a deep well.

woken up on a Monday morning and then before you know it, it is Friday night, you are sitting over a pint of beer, a Gin and Tonic or a glass or wine and realising that you have just 'lived' or 'lost' five days of your life?!

Waking hours
Let's say 7am – 11pm = 16 waking hours a day
9 – 5 job = 8 hrs a day
229 working days a year x 8 hours a day = 1832 working hours
And you also get 1832 hours NOT working!
BUT travelling to work - 2 hrs = 458 hrs per year
Leaving 1374 hours of our OWN TIME during a working week!

Waking hours for a year = 5840
Work 1832 =31%
Travel 458 = 7%
Free time during working week 1374 = 23%
Weekends - 52 weeks x 2 days x 16 waking hours – 1664 = 28%
Holidays and Festivals = 11%

Therefore, if we are looking to take control of our life, we have the freedom of choice to decide WHAT to do in 69% of our life! Naturally enough, in theory, we have the choice with what we do with 100% of our life. But bear in mind I am focusing on what we can do outside the confines of a job.

Let's call this 'Grab Back'. By the way, I appreciate that with flexi hours and flexible hours of working this

> It's always too soon to quit.
>
> *David T Scoates*

NOTES:

'I am planning, with a sense of reality and necessity for all my weekends'

He couldn't remember quite how he had got there, or how long he had been sitting in the dark, damp, miserable lonely place…

'grab back the weekend' concept could be applied to grabbing back your time off!

We can attack Grab Back in the following areas:
Weekends – 28%
Travel – 7%
Free time during working week – 23%
Holidays – 11%

We have looked at one area – Weekends. But we could adopt the same plan/attitude/focus on the other 3 areas. Funnily enough we could even see if we are allowed a lunch hour! What would happen then?!

Weekend cherishing

I ponder upon these times a great deal. In fact one **fear** I had was not living and cherishing the moment, of stopping to be aware, of breathing in the experience, of being there, in the present, where I am. It is a habit to be mastered and it is to be practiced and practiced and practiced. I started these habits years ago. My first step was to have a weekend journal which allows me to take stock of each weekend; it helps me to do two things - plan the weekend, and make the most of it, but also the opportunity to reflect back at the past weeks and remind myself of the journey.

So the fear I am alluding to is the fear of life whistling by; (because it can be as fast or as slow as you want it to be), allowing it to rush by without picking the fruits of joy from it along the way. I must confess to enjoying Facebook these days, having 'discovered' it finally in

> **In all human affairs there are efforts, and there are results, and the strength of the effort is the measure of the result.**
> *James Allen*

NOTES:

I use my time wisely, my time is more precious than anything.

but he vaguely remembered once being told of a beautiful world near an ocean with bountiful food supplies, comfortable shelter and plenty of friends; in fact the perfect "frog environment".

September 2010. The reason I like it is daft. Even though some people may see it as boring and self indulgent, it is nice to see people sharing what they are going to do and indeed, saying how it went! They are pausing, taking stock and reviewing. A healthy habit.

So where does the **weekend journal** fit into the big scheme of things? Well it is just another little habit or tool, call it what you will. It is an A5 diary, it is a mind map and it is the habit of crafting a weekend, rather than letting the weekend wash over you. By all means fill it with courses, life activities, parties, events, sport, workshops, seminars, concerts etc. But if you consider this, for a great number of individuals the weekend is a major element of one's life. Fifty-two weeks a year so one hundred and four days a year, sixteen hours awake-time per day (if you sleep the normal eight hours a night), so that is one thousand six hundred and sixty-four hours to be crafted, cherished and enjoyed.

Weekends are 28% or your time – 104 days/365 = 28%
6 days at Xmas and 6 days at Easter = 12 days/365 = 3%
4 weeks holiday is 20 days/365 = 5%
Work 229 days/365 = 62%

And can be represented by the graph overleaf:

> **Genius is the ability to reduce the complicated to the simple.**
>
> *C. W. Ceran*

NOTES:

I have plenty of time, all is going according to plan.

He thought he had been heading for this world but had ended up in the well instead…

My year

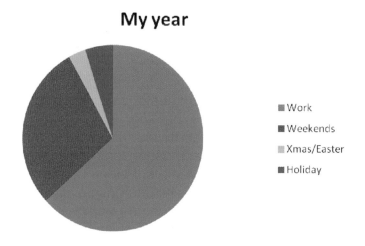

- Work
- Weekends
- Xmas/Easter
- Holiday

NOTES:

I have seen the weekend considered in a variety of ways. Some people for example map out their weekends into six quadrants – AM; PM; EVE, some map it out into eight quadrants. Of course there are 'busy weekends', 'away weekends' and 'down time' weekends. By 'down' I don't plan to be mellow for forty-eight hours, I mean a 'chill out' weekend. In my family we always come out with the phrase 'what is the agenda?' there is no 'agenda' if nothing is planned that particular weekend. Ok if this suits you and doesn't strike you as too analytical, and then try it. The objective is to relax, do the things you want to do, with a balance of family and relationship time, with chores, reading and fun etc. It can of course be fun to plan a great weekend. It must **never** be a pressure and if a spontaneous event takes over, so be it - let it be!

Weekends can be divided into 6 quadrants:

I have fulfilling weekends full of memorable moments.

...There was very little to eat in the well, and because the frog was a great risk-analyst he worked out that he could survive indefinitely on a daily basis

	Saturday	Sunday
A.M.		
P.M.		
Eve		

Or 8 quadrants:

	Saturday	Sunday
Early A.M.		
Lunch 12 - 2		
P.M.		
Eve		

Weekends can be planned ahead thus:

January
Weekend No 1 (chillout weekend)
Weekend No 2 (weekend away)
Weekend No 3 (seminar)
Weekend No 4 (people staying)

February
Weekend No 5 (weekend away)
Weekend No 6 (1 day seminar/1 day off)
Weekend No 7 (chillout weekend)
Weekend No 8 (Visitors/Rugby match)
Etc...

We have not addressed the rest of your life spinning past, but at least we have placed a stake in the ground and decided to 'take back' our weekends. Enjoy them

I love planning my weekends.

...by staying where he was and conserving his energy.

He who wishes to secure the good of others has already secured his own.

Confucius

NOTES:

and reflect upon them. Wow! What is exciting once this little method is practiced and mastered is it takes no time. But you can then go one step further!

You could try looking at your weekend and seeing if anything in your goal planning needs to be improved or added into your weekend. For example one of my goals in 2010 was to play the guitar more, because I am well aware that when I sit down and play the guitar I relax. I know that if I play the guitar it is good for my creative mind and it is great for reaching a zone of 'time out'. When I am playing the guitar and singing it is difficult to think about anything else. So it is a great method of applying the 'when you are there, be there' rule.

So in my weekend schedule I always have guitar time there for me to look at – it is not the end of the world if I do not get round to playing every weekend, but it happens as the result of a conscious plan or intention. This concept which we all know well: having no time. But is it really that we have no time or could we attempt a little gentle planning to *make* the time? Could we build in elements of our life, or as in my case, build parts of our life back in which we once loved and included, or new aspects which we would like to include! Painting, reading, poetry, walking, holding hands with your loved one.

I used to play the guitar a lot, in fact I think the count of songs written is up to about 200 plus, but I do not play much anymore. Why? I do not know; I never seem to have the time! Look I am **not** saying your weekends have to be planned to the minute. But what

> **Thinking is the hardest work there is, which is the probably reason why so few engage in it.**
>
> *Henry Ford*

NOTES:

I have plenty of time to follow my passions.

At least he was safe.

I am suggesting is that you consider honoring your time; take ten minutes out to plan your weekend. Consider if you can weave some of your goals into your weekend. It helps give a sense of direction and a sense of fun and it certainly helps completely remove the horrible fear people have that 'life is passing me by'. It is a very common one!

So we have addressed one or two little methods or tools to protect against the fear of letting the world roll all over you and tumble you around like a pebble on the beach! You are now able to put a stake in the ground and say to yourself "NO, I like my life with purpose and direction!" This is a great feeling and it creates more confidence and happiness as well as casting off the fears, of all kinds, that can weigh us down.

"I am stuck in a rut!" "I never seem to get things done!" "My life is not my own!" These are all self-limiting beliefs of course but underpinned by the sense of non-achievement, non-fulfillment or of being stuck. Naturally enough these self-limiting beliefs are a great power within all of us and we have to work against these with energy and passion. Let me expand upon that. Let's say we haven't been taking control of our weekends for some years, but we make a decision to adopt the tool of planning areas of our weekend with a mind map or the quadrant idea. Well let me encourage realistic expectations here. Unless you are superhuman it will not be perfect from the start and it certainly will not work like clockwork immediately!

> **There's a level of you that has to be OK no matter how things turn out, because the universe doesn't work with desperation.**
>
> *Oprah Winfrey*

NOTES:

My life is exciting and fulfilling.

Or, he could use up all of his energy in making a mighty effort to jump out and see if his "Frog Nirvana" was really there.

My weekend planner (filled in) – you can create your own blank:

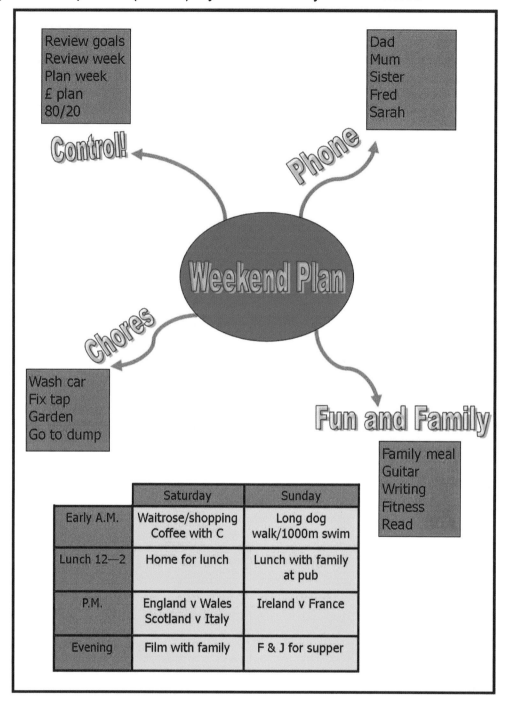

Control!
Review goals
Review week
Plan week
£ plan
80/20

Phone
Dad
Mum
Sister
Fred
Sarah

Weekend Plan

Chores
Wash car
Fix tap
Garden
Go to dump

Fun and Family
Family meal
Guitar
Writing
Fitness
Read

	Saturday	Sunday
Early A.M.	Waitrose/shopping Coffee with C	Long dog walk/1000m swim
Lunch 12—2	Home for lunch	Lunch with family at pub
P.M.	England v Wales Scotland v Italy	Ireland v France
Evening	Film with family	F & J for supper

There is the concept of the twenty-one day habit! But of course we are jumping five days at a time, skipping your working week. Most coaches recommend that it takes 21 days/times to *make* a habit and 21 days/times to *break* a habit. It is suggested that if you adopt a habit after 21 days/times your body and mind is then programmed to handle this new habit.

So the twenty-one day/time concept to break a habit or create a new one will not necessarily work here. Ok, well, we will simply adapt some decisive tools. We want to cherish weekends; we therefore decide to adapt the mind map plan each weekend. We need to lay out a plan to 'make it happen'. How about drawing out your mind map, then printing it out thirteen times. Thirteen times because, of course thirteen weeks at ninety days is quarter of the year. Find an old diary, A5 or A4 it doesn't matter, and as you go through the quarter add a plan for each weekend, then stick it into your diary, live your weekend and bingo!

Your measure of success for your self-acceptability is that you have thirteen weekend mind maps stuck into your diary and you have the ability to reflect back on your weekends, to see that you have now adopted the habit. Thirteen weekends, (no, I do not believe 13 is an unlucky number), is perfect as well. I come from a sales background originally and thirteen weeks was a great length of time for mapping out good sales targets. You assume that whatever you want to achieve can be done over ten weeks, you then have 1/13 to take time off to celebrate and you have 2/13 weeks to account for things getting in the way such as a cold, the flu or family issues. So in effect you are adopting a method which anticipates the inevitable 'things will never go according to plan!'

> **Follow your bliss. If you are on your own path then things will come to you.**
>
> *Susan Sarendon*

NOTES:

I love my life! I am happy and contented.

But what if it wasn't?

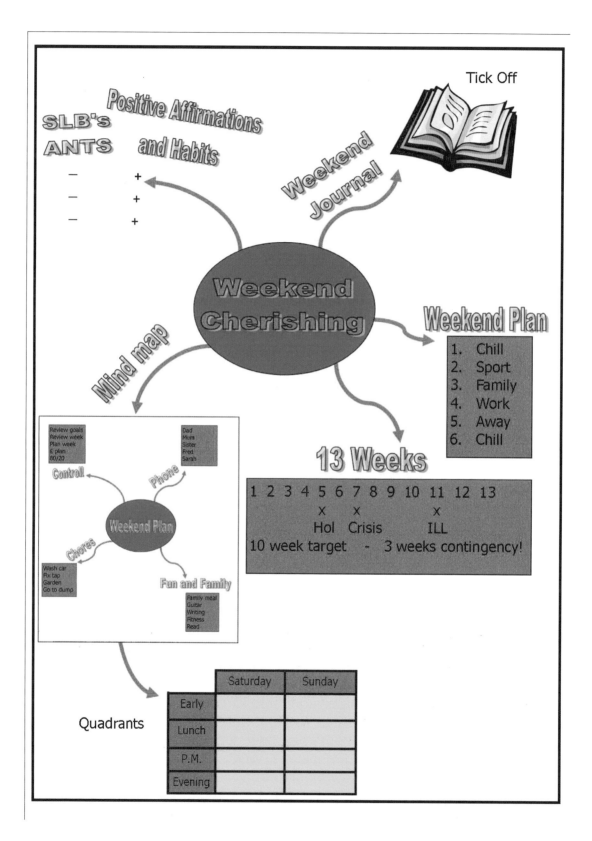

Step Up and FOCUS

This gives you the comfort of knowing that you are allowed to 'mess up'; to miss a week; to forget and still allow you to keep up. For the perfectionists amongst you – congratulations! But for us mere mortals, this is a logical way to move forward. I do this, it works!

What I am saying is, it is ok to adapt the 'take back my weekends' success habit and it is OK to achieve 10/13 mind maps over a quarter. You will be creating a change in your life and still need to be fighting the tide of fears that go with phrases like...

- "I am so disorganised!"
- "I would love to....!"
- "I wish I could......!"

Let's recap on these SLB's (Self Limiting Beliefs) by the way. We have 40,000 automatic negative thoughts or SLB's floating through our brains during the working hours of each day.

So in my case, at the tender age of 52, (let's assume my first five years of my life were positive, therefore that leaves 47 years) that is:

47 years x 365 days x 40,000 limiting thoughts a day = **686,200,000** negative thoughts through my lifetime!

Here you are, trying to create an element of change, but your subconscious mind is not accepting it. I do not blame it, the evidence is too strong in favour of 'this is the way it is,' 'You cannot possibly change now!' 'A leopard cannot change its spots!' etc.

> **Be kind, for everyone you meet is fighting a harder battle.**
>
> *Plato*

NOTES:

Every minute of my day is precious and I enjoy it all.

The moral of this story can be interpreted in many ways, but for me it is saying two things,
1. A little belief can go a long way – there may be a very beautiful life very close to us but because we are comfortable we can't see it and we may never know that it is there.

BUT, by taking positive actions with a clear and assured self-accountability measure – your mindset **can** change. Your desire and ultimately your results based on the action you have taken will win the day. Your SLB's can't argue with the facts.

I play the guitar regularly to relax and the chance to really, really relax and create is important to me. This is an affirmation I can use and it resonates with my subconscious because it is now true! Do I play enough? Still not enough but it has a place in my weekend agenda and it is more likely to happen these days than some many years before, when the only time I played guitar was during long lingering holidays in France.

I know that all this seems very logical but the simple fact is that these tiny inner battles we all have against fear or other issues in our mind are very real and can be combated with a little success habit modeling.

Chapter 7 Summary

I have taken you through one small element of grabbing back time and your life for at least one third of the year, the weekends. If and when you apply this strategy or methodology, even if you have a full-on 40-60 hour week, Monday to Friday, you can still take control of your life, have your own personal goals and achieve them. If you can achieve this for

> **By discussion comes understanding; by understanding comes light; by light comes wisdom; by wisdom comes life.**
> *Maori Proverb*

NOTES:

I am excited about my present and my future.

2. If life is not good then something much change, even if it means a huge effort with no guaranteed results.

weekends, think what else you can do! You can actually apply the same principles to the whole of your life.

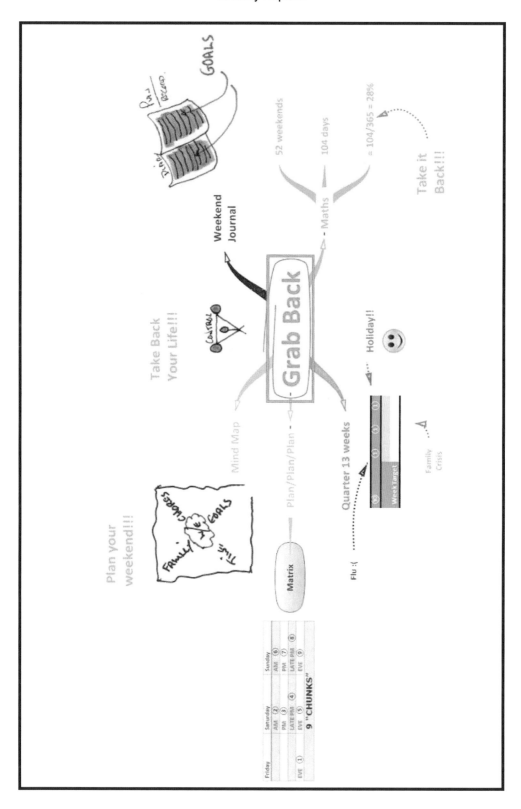

Conclusion

I have given you a glimpse of my world and a selection of what I call 'success habits' or 'handrails of success'. They have helped me a great deal and what I have shared with you in this book is a collation of a whole series of tools used in different areas which I have tried out, modified and then adopted as part of my life. There is a logical progression to being the best you can be, living life on purpose and to the full. I cannot kid you and suggest that it is anything other than hard work.

You will need to apply yourself and stick to it. You may try a few things and then forget and so the key is to have a *review date* for each little adventure or habit change you have tried and a record of how it's gone. If you forget, get distracted or have one priority jump the queue and usurp your original goal, don't panic! Simply try again!

I have shared with you my story "since the age of 23" and the advice I would give the 23 year old knowing what I know now. I have also shared with you the 10 Success Habits that I have found to be vital for me and I hope these will be useful to you. If you are striving to be successful, whatever that may mean to you, you must accept that it is necessary to maintain a continuous vigilance and active review of your progress and continually refine the tools and success habits to help you move forward.

I have presented you with what I see as the natural stages of creating the building blocks to your accelerated performance. All you need to do now is implement some or all of them!

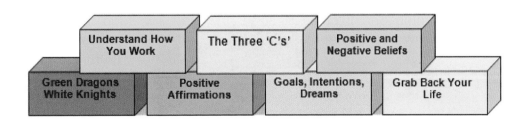

What next?

Well I think the first thing I have to do is compliment you on reading my book. It sends all sorts of messages if you have purchased or borrowed this book. It means you want to 'step up'; it means you want to improve your life and the pace of the journey you are on; it means you are on the great quest for self-improvement.

When I read a personal development book I tend to do so 'actively' and take the following approach :-

- I speed read the book/or skim through it at outset.
- I sign and date the front of the book to take "ownership".
- I use sticky notes and highlighter pens to mark key points that I deem important.
- I also keep a book journal which I use as a reference book and I mind map the book.

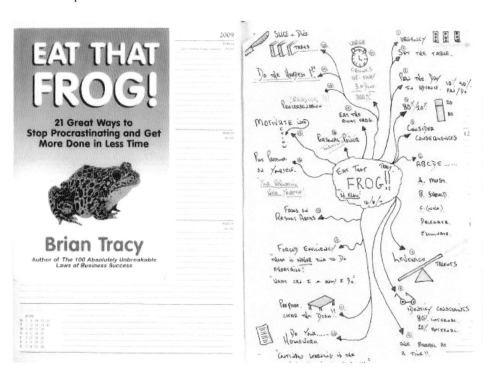

A page from my Book Journal

So there you are, you have spent a few hours of your life with this book. We have to ask the question:-

NOW WHAT?

I believe you have some questions to ask or decisions to make:-

1. Shall I use some of the information and try some of the ideas outlined in this book to help me?
2. Great read but I shall do nothing with this information.
3. Great read and I will come back to it one day.

Any of the 3 decisions is fine with me, it's your life! But if your decision is Number 1, then my advice is to spend 20/30 minutes and take this time to decide how much, of what, and by when, will you apply this knowledge.

Action Plan

What are you going to do?   How much?   By when?   Review when?

1.
2.
3.
4.
5.

You may wish to engage a friend/buddy to help you with this and to call you to prompt you every couple of weeks and ask you how it's going, calling you to account.

I understand that a self-help book, a positive mind feed book or a personal development book will help simply by reading it and doing nothing. The message will be retained in your subconscious and you will apply some of the ideas, of that I am sure!

However, as my PA commented "But if I actually wish to do something what shall I do now?". So if you wish to take decision No. 1, you need to map out an Action Plan to weave this learning into your life to help you improve and move towards successfully achieving your goals faster. I have made this step easier for you!

I have mapped out three examples of how you can apply this learning. You review the book briefly, Chapter by Chapter and pull out the action you wish to apply to you. You can't do everything so I have chosen 7 Actions for you.

Once you have seen my examples, have a go and make this book come alive for you!

Example I

No.	Chapter No.	What?	How?	By When?
1.	1	Ask 5 friends for opinion of me	Using Johari Window idea	2 weeks time
2.	2	Have a look at my 5 fears	Understand them, take action to remove them	Over next 3 months
3.	3	Have a look and identify	3 self-limiting patterns I have	Over next 3 months
4.	4	Identify my top 5	Green Dragons	This week!
5.	5	Do an Affirmation Card set	Affirmations to link to goals.	Today
6.	6	Re-do my goals	10 goals for this year	2 weeks time
7.	7	Start one!	Weekend Journal	This weekend

Example II

No.	Chapter No.	What?	How?	By When?
1.	Introduction	Write my new story	2000 words	1 months time
2.	10 Key Learning Points	Adopt these ideas	10 steps	Immediately!
3.	1	Do my own profile owl/dolphin etc.	Use it to play to my strengths	This weekend
4.	2	Start to be aware of my own confidence	Ask friends/get feedback	Over 2 months
5.	3	Stop self limiting phases	Ask mates to pull me up on these	Immediately!

| 6. | 7 | Look at the maths to do with my life | Work out how much time I waste/Could use | Today |
| 7. | 7 | Look at my weekends | Plan a variety of adventure weekends with the family | Next weekend |

Example III

No.	Chapter No.	What?	How?	By When?
1.	10 Key Learning Point	Study the 80/20 Rule	Get and read both books by Koch	Over next 2 months
2.	1	Work on the intelligences	Take my scores, make an Action Plan	Next week
3.	2	Get a coach	To improve. To overcome fears	Within 4 weeks
4.	3	Create my own Daily Set Up	Develop a 20 minute me-time daily	Straight away
5.	4	Speak to best friend/ 'buddy'	On stopping self limiting phrases	Next week!
6.	6	Re-plan my goals	Place goals on fridge	Within 2 months
7.	7	Plan my weekends	Get a weekend journal	Now!

No.	Chapter No.	What?	How?	By When?
1.				
2.				
3.				
4.				
5.				
6.				
7.				
8.				
9.				
10.				

If you want stronger guidance from a professional you may even want to look at my web site www.futureperformancecoaching.com and enlist my help or the help of my team of superb coaches on a programme of face to face coaching, phone coaching or a mixture of the two. Or indeed you may simply e-mail me personally *(Lindsay@trafalgarsq.co.uk)* and be placed on an alert list for when I am running a workshop or seminar and come and meet me which would be a delight, indeed!

I am on what is known as the 'property network circuit' in the UK which is, as you now know, where I first started on the coaching journey that I am still on. So if you search for your local property network meeting in your town or city I am bound to turn up and meet you at some stage soon. My itinerary is up-dated on the web site www.futureperformancecoaching.com regularly.

You will also see that I produce a series of affirmation CD's which are based on helping you kick-start the day and they help with your 'daily set up'. The feedback I get from this CD is that they really do help, so you may wish to try one out.

Whatever happens enjoy the 'step up' and enjoy the thrill and pure adrenalin rush involved when you

F.O.C.U.S – Follow One Course Until Successful.

Recommended Reading and References

My Book List by Author, Year, *Title* , Publisher

Adams, Scott, 2002, *Another Day in Cubic Paradise*, Dilbert
Adewale, Micheal, 2008*, Class Dismissed*, Micheal Adewale
Aldows, Hugh, 1983, *How to set up & run your own business*, Daily Telegraph
Bamford, Martin , 2006, *The Money Tree*, Pearson
Blanchard, K; Bowles, S, 1998, *Gung Ho!*, Harper Collins
Blanchard, K; Bowles, S, 1998, *Raving Fans!,* Harper Collins
Blanchard; Zigarmi; Zigarmi, 1985, *Leadership & the One Minute Manager*, Fontana/Collins
Borg, James, 2004, *Persuasion*, Pearson
Breithaupt, Tim, 1999, *10 Steps to Sales Success*, Amacom
Buchrach, Bill, 2000, *Values-Based Financial Planning*, Aim High
Buzan, Tony, 1971, *The Speed Reading Book*, BBC
Buzan, Tony, 2001, *Head Strong*, Thorsons
Canfield; Hansen; Hewitt, 2000, *The Power of Focus*, Vermillion
Carlon, Richard, 2002, *What About the Big Stuff*, Positive
Chapman, G; Campbell, R., 2005, *The Five Love Languages of Children*, Northfield Publishing
Chapman, Gary, 2010, *The 5 Love Languages*, Northfield Publishing
Clayton, Mike, 2011, *Brilliant Stress Management*, Pearson
Collins, Jim, 2009*, How to the Mighty Fall and Why Some Companies Never Give In*, Ransom House
Cope, Mike, 2010, *The Secrets of Success in Coaching* , Pearson
Davidson, Jeff, 2000, *Project Management*, Alpha
de Bono, Edward , 1971, *Lateral Thinking of Management*, Penguin
de Bono, Edward, 1985, *Six Thinking Hats,* Penguin
de Bono, Edward , 1985, *Tactics*, Fontana
Ditzler, Jinny, 1994, *Your Best Year Yet*, Thorsons
Dr Batra, Ravi, 1988, *The Great Depression of 1990*, Bantam
Dr Briers, Stephen, 2009*, Brilliant Cognitive Behavioural Therapy*, Pearson
Dr Kashel, Gerald , 1984, *The 4%* , Sidgwick & Jackson
Dr Miller, Liz, 2009, *Mood Mapping*, Rodale
Eysenck, H; Wilson, G, 1975, *Know Your Own Personality*, Book Club Associates
Farell, Dominic, 2006, *The Jet-to-Let Bible*, Lawpack
Ferguson, Marc, 1995, *Sales Esteem*, Pax
Ferriss, Timothy, 2007, *The 4-Hour Week*, Vermillion
Freemantle, David, 2004, *The Buzz*, Nicholas Brealey
Gallo, Carmine, 2010, *The Presentation Secrets of Steve Jobs*, McGraw-Hill
Gerber, Michael E., 1995, *The E Myth*, Harper Collins
Gitomer, Jeffrey, 2007, *Little Green Book of Getting Your Way*, FT Press
Gitomer, Jeffrey, 2007, *Little Platinum Book of Cha-Ching!,* FT Press
Gitomer, Jeffrey, 2007, *Little Gold Book of Yes! Attitude*, FT Press
Gladwell, Malcolm, 2005, *Blink*, Penguin
Gladwell, Malcom, 2008*, Outliers*, Penguin
Gladwell, Malcom, 2000, *The Tipping Point*, Abacus
Goldratt, E. M; Cox, J., 1984, *The Goal*, Gower
Grieve, Bradley T., 2008, *Thank You for Being You*, BTG Studios
Hamilton, Roger, 2006, *Your Life Your Legacy*, Achievers
Hancock, Jonathan, 2011, *Brilliant Memory Training*, Pearson

Hardy, Darren, 2010, *The Compound Effect*, Success
Harv Eker, T., 1996, *Speedwealth*, Peak Potentials
Harv Eker, T., 2005, *Secrets of the Millionaire Mind: Mastering the Inner Game of Wealth*, Harper Collins
Heller, Robert, 2001, *Managing for Excellence*, Dorling Kindersley
Hicks, Esher & Jerry, 2006, *The Secret Law of Attraction*, Hay House
Hicks, Esher & Jerry, 2008, *Money and the Law of Attraction*, Hay House
Hill, Napoleon, 1966, *Think and Grow Rich*, Wilshire Books
Hill, Napoleon, 1995, *Positive Action Plan*, Piatkus
Hodgkinson, Liz, 2006, *The Complete Guide to Investing in Property*, Kogan
Jay, Ros, 1995, *How to Build a Great Team*, Prentice Hall
Johnson, Kerry L., 1993, *Selling with NLP*, Positive
Kaplun, R. S; Norton, D. P, 2004, *Strategy Maps*, HBS Press
Kellaway, Lucy, 2007, *The Answers*, Profile
Kiyosaki, Robert , 2000, *Rich Dad Poor Dad*, Sphere
Kiyosaki, Robert , 2000, *Rich Dad's Guide to Investing*, Timewarner
Koch, Richard, 2004, *Living the 80/20 way*, Nicholas Brealey
Koch, Richard, 1997, *The 80/20 Principle*, Nicholas Brealey
Krause, Donald G., 1996, *Sun Tzu: The Art of War for Executives*, Nicholas Brealey
Krogerus; Tschappler, 2011, *The Decision Book*, Pearson
Larson Alan, 2003, *Demystifying Six Sigma*, Amacom
Le Boeuf, Micheal, 1986, *How to Motivate People*, Sidwick & Jackson
Leigh, Andrew , 2008, *The Charisma Effect*, Pearson
Leighton; Kilbey; Bill, 2011, *101 Days to Make a Change: Daily Strategies to Move from Knowing to Being,* Crown House
Livingston, I; Thomson, J, 2007, *Train Your Brain in Seven Days*, Icon
Martin, Curly, 2001, *The Life Coaching Handbook*, Crown House
Matthews, Dan, 2007, *Starting & Running a Business All in One for Dummies*, Mattews
Maxwell, John C., 2003, *Thinking for a Change*, Warner
Mayne, Brian, 2006, *Goal Mapping*, Watkins
McConnell, 2005, *Make Money Be Happy*, Pearson
McCormack, Mark H., 1984, *What They Don't Teach You at Harvard Business School*, Collins
McIntosh, Ron, 1993, *The Greatest Secret*, White Stone
McKenna, Paul, 2006, *90 Day Success Journal*, Bantam
Milligan, A; Smith, S, 2006, *See Feel Think Do*, Marshall Cavendish
Mullingan, Eileen, 1999, *Life Coaching Change Your Life in 7 Days*, Piatkus
O'Connell, Fergus, 2008, *How to Get More Done*, Pearson
Olson, Jeff, 2005, *The Slight Edge*, Success
Owen, Jo, 2010, *How to Tell*, Prentice Hall
Owen, Nick, 2004, *More Magic of Metaphors*, Crown House
Owen, Nick, 2004, *The Magic of Metaphors*, Crown House
Ozaniec, Naomi, 1997, *101 Essential Tips: Everyday Meditation*, Dorling Kindersley
Parkes Cordock, R, 2006, *Millionaire Upgrade*, Capstone
Parkin, John C., 2007, *Fuck It*, Hay House
Pease, Allan & Barbara , 2004, *The Definitive Book of Body Language*, Orion
Peck, M. Scott, 1990, *The Road Less Travelled*, Arrow
Peeling, Nic, 2005, *Brilliant Manager*, Pearson
Periklis, Mark, 2010, *The Insiders Guide to Buying Property in Difficult Times*, Filament
Richardson, Pam, 2004, *Life Coach*, Hamlyn
Roberts, Graham, 2003, *Law Relating to Financial Services*, IFS
Rowntree, Derek, 1996, *The Manager's Book of Checklists*, Pearson
Searle, Sue, 2012, *Affirmations for Success*, Amazon

Senge, Peter M., 1990, *The Fifth Discipline*, Century Business
Silbinger, Steven, 1999, *The 10-Day MBA*, Piatkus
Streibel, Barbara J., 2003, *The Manager's Guide to Effective Meetings*, Briefcase
Strutely, Richard, 1999, *The Definitive Business Plan*, Prentice Hall
Templar, Richard, 2005, *The Rules of Management*, Pearson
Thaler, R. H; Sunstein, C. R, 2008, *Nudge*, Caravan
Tom, D; Barrons, B. R., 2006, *The Business General: Transform your business using seven secrets of military success*, Vermillion
Tracy, Brian, 2001, *Eat That Frog*, Berret Koehler
Turner, Catherine, 2001, *Personal Lending & Mortgages*, Financial World
Turner, Colin, 1997, *Swimming with Piranha makes you Hungry*, InToto
Turner, Colin, 1994, *Born to Succeed*, Element
Vickers; Bavister; Smith, 2009, *Personal Impact*, Pearson
Virtue, Doreen, 2006, *Angels 101*, Hay House
Virtue, Doreen, 2007, *How to Hear Your Angels*, Hay House
von Oech, Roger , 1983, *A Whack on the side of the Head*, Hachette
von Senger, Harro, 2004, *The 36 Strategies of Business*, Marshall Cavendish
Walsh, Ciaran, 1996*, Key Management Ratios*, Prentice Hall
Watkins, Micheal, 2003, *The First 90 Days*, HBS Press
Wattles, Wallace D., 1976, *The Science of Getting Rich*, Destiny
Webb, Phillip & Sandra, 1999, *The Small Business Handbook*, Prentice Hall
Welch, Jack, 2005, *Winning*, Harper Collins
Welch, Suzy, 2009, *10 Minutes 10 Months 10 Years: A Life Transforming Idea*, Simon & Schuster
Whitmore, John, 1992, *Coaching for Performance*, Nicholas Brealey
Whitney, Russ, 1984, *Overcoming*, Whitney Leadership Group
Whitney, Russ, 1995, *Building Wealth*, Fireside
Williams, Nick, 1999, *The Work We Were Born To Do*, Element
Wilson, Derek, 1988, *Rothschild* , Andre Deutch
Wiseman, Richard, 2003, *The Luck Factor*, Arrow
Wood, Frank, 1967, *Business Accounting 1*, Prentice Hall
Yeung, Rob, 2008, *Confidence*, Pearson
Yeung, Rob, 2009, *Personality*, Pearson

Made in the USA
Charleston, SC
09 April 2014